THE 2019 SOLO AND SMALL FIRM LEGAL TECHNOLOGY GUIDE

ABA LAW PRACTICE DIVISION
The Business of Practicing Law

THE 2019 SOLO AND SMALL FIRM LEGAL TECHNOLOGY GUIDE

SHARON D. NELSON, JOHN W. SIMEK,
AND MICHAEL C. MASCHKE

Cover design by Tahiti Spears/ABA Design.

Printed in the United States of America.

23 22 21 20 19   5 4 3 2 1

ISBN: 978-1-64105-375-4

Discounts are available for books ordered in bulk. Special consideration is given to state bars, CLE programs, and other bar-related organizations. Inquire at Book Publishing, ABA Publishing, American Bar Association, 321 N. Clark Street, Chicago, Illinois 60654-7598.

www.ShopABA.org

Dedication

Sharon Nelson and John Simek dedicate this book to their children, Kelly, Sara, Kim, JJ, Jason, and Jamie, and to their grandchildren, Samantha, Tyler, Lilly, Henry, Evan, Jordan, Cash, Parker, and Philippa. May the adventures with all of you continue!

Michael Maschke dedicates this book to his wife, Summer, and three wonderful children, Lily, Sutton, and Harrison. I am so blessed to have you all in my life.

Contents at a Glance

Table of Contents

About the Authors

Sharon D. Nelson, Esq.

Sharon D. Nelson is the president of Sensei Enterprises, Inc. Ms. Nelson graduated from Georgetown University Law Center in 1978 and has been in private practice ever since. She now focuses exclusively on cybersecurity and digital forensics.

Ms. Nelson, Mr. Simek, and Mr. Maschke are the co-authors of the eleven previous editions of this book (2008–2018). Ms. Nelson and Mr. Simek are also co-authors (with David Ries) of *Locked Down: Practical Information Security for Lawyers* (American Bar Association, 2nd ed. 2016, 1st edition published in 2012) and *Encryption Made Simple for Lawyers* (American Bar Association, 2015). Additionally, Ms. Nelson and Mr. Simek are co-authors of *The Electronic Evidence and Discovery Handbook: Forms, Checklists, and Guidelines* (ABA, 2006). Ms. Nelson is a co-author of *How Good Lawyers Survive Bad Times* (ABA, 2009). Ms. Nelson and Mr. Simek's articles have appeared in numerous national publications, and they frequently lecture throughout the country on digital forensics and legal technology subjects.

Ms. Nelson is a co-host of Legal Talk Network's *The Digital Edge: Lawyers and Technology* and *Digital Detectives* podcasts. Ms. Nelson and Mr. Simek have a regular legal tech column called "Hot Buttons" in the ABA Law Practice Division magazine *Law Practice*. Ms. Nelson was a member of the American Bar Association's Cybersecurity Task Force, and serves on its Standing Committee on Technology and Information Systems. She serves on the governing Council of the Law Practice Division and as a Law Practice Scholar.

Ms. Nelson is a Past President of the Virginia State Bar (2013–14). She is a past president of the Fairfax Bar Association and past president of the Fairfax Law Foundation, past chair of the ABA's TECHSHOW Board, and past chair of the ABA's Law Practice Management Publishing Board and its Professional Development Board. She is a graduate of Leadership Fairfax and served for many years on the Governing Council of the Virginia State Bar and on its Executive Committee. She is the former chair of the Virginia State Bar's Unauthorized Practice of Law Committee and served on both its Technology Committee and its Standing Committee on Finance. She is currently the chair of the Virginia State Bar's Future of Law Practice Committee, its Better Annual Meeting Committee, and the VSB TECHSHOW 2019. She is a member of the ABA, the Virginia Bar, the Virginia Bar Association, the Virginia Trial Lawyers Association, the Virginia Women Lawyers Association, and the Fairfax Bar Association.

Ms. Nelson was inducted into the College of Law Practice Management in 2014 and currently serves on its Board of Trustees and served as the Co-Chair of the 2017 and 2018 Futures Conference.

In 2015, Ms. Nelson was named by *Virginia Lawyers Weekly* as a member of the Class of 2015's Leaders in the Law. This honor recognizes attorneys and professionals in law-related fields who made outstanding contributions to the practice of law in Virginia, significant achievements through the practice of law, leadership in improving the justice system, and important contributions to Virginia's legal community and/or the community at large.

Ms. Nelson served as a Court Appointed Special Advocate (CASA) for Abused and Neglected Children for five years.

John W. Simek

John W. Simek is the vice president of Sensei Enterprises, Inc. He is a Certified Information Systems Security Professional (CISSP) and a nationally known testifying expert in the area of digital forensics. Mr. Simek holds a degree in engineering from the United States Merchant Marine Academy and an MBA in finance from Saint Joseph's University. Before forming Sensei, he was a senior technologist with Mobil Oil Corporation for more than 20 years, troubleshooting and designing Mobil's networks throughout the Western Hemisphere.

In addition to his CISSP designation, Mr. Simek is an EnCase Certified Examiner (EnCE), Certified Handheld Examiner, a Certified Novell Engineer, Microsoft Certified Professional + Internet, Microsoft Certified Systems Engineer, NT Certified Independent Professional, and a Certified Internetwork Professional. He is also a member of the High Tech Crime Network, the Fairfax Bar Association, and the American Bar Association. In addition to co-authoring the books cited in Ms. Nelson's biography, he also serves as the Co-Chair of the 2019 ABA TECHSHOW planning board of the Law Practice Division. He also serves as a Board Member of the Virginia Law Foundation. He currently provides information technology support to hundreds of area law firms, legal entities, and corporations. He lectures on legal technology, cybersecurity, and digital forensics subjects throughout the world.

He is a co-host of Legal Talk Network's *Digital Detectives* podcast.

Mr. Simek also served as a Court Appointed Special Advocate (CASA) for Abused and Neglected Children for five years.

Michael C. Maschke

Michael Maschke is the Chief Executive Officer and a digital forensics examiner at Sensei Enterprises, Inc. He is a Certified Computer Examiner (CCE), an EnCase Certified forensic examiner (EnCE), Certified Ethical Hacker (CEH) and a Certified Information Systems Security Professional (CISSP).

Mr. Maschke holds a degree in telecommunications from James Madison University. He has significant experience with network troubleshooting, design and implementation, systems integration, and computer engineering. Prior to becoming the Chief Executive Officer, Mr. Maschke oversaw Sensei's information technology department, which provided support to hundreds of area law firms and corporations.

He has spoken at the American Bar Association's TECHSHOW conference on information security and is a co-author of *Information Security for Lawyers and Law Firms* as well as the last eleven editions of this book, all published by the American Bar Association.

Acknowledgments

Once again, we welcome our good friend Jim Calloway as the author of the introduction to this book. Jim is the director of the Oklahoma Bar Association's Management Assistance Program. He frequently writes and speaks on legal technology issues, internet research, law office management and organization, and legal ethics. He is often on the faculty with us at ABA TECHSHOW and is Sharon's co host on the Legal Talk Network's *Digital Edge: Lawyers and Technology* podcast.

Thanks to all the folks from Lachina Creative who did all typesetting, editing, and other tasks that go into a book like this. We appreciate how hard you all worked to get this book "on the streets" in time for the New Year and look forward to many years working together. We especially wish to thank Molly Montanaro, the Program Manager, and Morgan McClelland, our Project Manager.

On the ABA side, we thank Caroline Whiting, our marketing specialist—we appreciate all your hard work!

And thanks to Richard Ferguson, our long-time friend and once again Project Manager for this edition of the book. Richard, we will salute with a "wee dram" when we see the book in print! Thanks to Dave Ries for serving as our liaison to the Law Practice Publishing Board and to all of the Board members for their continuing support over many years!

Finally, we thank our colleagues here at Sensei, who carried the load while we were writing and were never too busy to deliberate over recommendations and to offer insightful comments. We don't come to work every day; we come to play, and we really like the folks we play with. Thanks, one and all!

Sharon Nelson, John Simek, Mike Maschke

Preface to the Twelfth Edition

What we hope to do with this book is simple: We want to help solo and small firm lawyers find the "sweet spot" of legal technology—the best value for the dollars. You don't need a yacht, and you won't be well served by a rowboat. But there is a happy medium—professional-grade hardware and software that doesn't cost an arm and a leg.

This guide is an annual one, so you can't go too far wrong with our advice. Some chapters will remain almost absolutely current. At worst, we'll only be several months behind the curve. Still, if you can't afford your own legal technology consultant and you are concerned about those who may be selling you snake oil, at least this book should provide you with an overview of recommended legal technology products for solo and small firm lawyers.

As always, the parts of this book that age quickly are the hardware specifications. We are happy to give you our latest specs—just drop us a quick line at sensei@senseient.com. We've given out hundreds of updated specs over the years, so don't hesitate to write!

We do our absolute best to be vendor-neutral. Readers of previous editions will be keenly aware that our advice has changed from year to year as some products excel and others decline—and sometimes precipitously. We have some exciting new products to talk about this year—nothing moves as fast as technology!

This is the only book we're aware of that deals with legal technology on a collective, annual basis. We seem to have a growing, loyal readership looking for independent advice on legal technology and find a yearly dose of that advice compelling.

This year, as we did last year, we have focused on the core technologies of the law office, opting to make the book more condensed and focused. The feedback from last year's changes has been very good with readers welcoming a more compact book focused on the essentials of legal tech—and finding it much easier to read.

Our recommendations are what we would do in a solo or small practice ourselves: Invest in quality technology that will have a good shelf life and serve you well—that means buying business-grade (not consumer-grade) technology. And don't expect more than the machines can give. A server can be expected to last four to five years; a workstation or laptop, three to four. That's it, folks. As the software also evolves, it demands ever more resources, and the hardware ages both physically and in its ability to handle the new software. Remember the Rule of Three in upgrading: You should be upgrading one-third of your technology each year. Sometimes you can stretch it to four years, but if you try to limp along patching things with spit and promises, you are likely going to be in for a "big bang" upgrade, which is acutely painful to the average solo or small law firm. Leasing may help lessen this financial burden (at least on an annual basis), but you lose the option to change course quickly without paying penalty fees.

Be mindful of the fact that this book is written exclusively for solos and small law firms. There is no attempt to include big-firm products or solutions, though many big-firm lawyers have enjoyed portions of this book. In addition, we want to stress that we have included only our recommendations, not all available products. If you don't see a product here, it is because that product is not among our usual recommendations. This is a best-of-breed selection to keep you from being confused by the veritable cornucopia of choices that exist. No one has time to wade through all the choices, so we've tried to give you limited but tested options that work.

We will repeat these words later in the book, but they are worth repeating here:

In some of our software descriptions, we are very critical of vendors who do not post pricing—they generally want to get you on the phone with someone from the sales department or give you an online demo, when all you want, in the beginning of your research, is some basic knowledge of features and pricing.

In the absence of pricing transparency by vendors, we encourage our readers to seek input from lawyers who actually use the products you are considering. Request specific references from vendors (though remember that those are likely to be cherry-picked!) and follow up on them. You will generally get some of the best counsel from practice management advisors. Listservs can be very helpful, as can local law practice management groups of state or local bar associations.

We used to say that generally we couldn't serve as your legal technology consultant unless you were in the D.C. area, but we are now providing managed IT (information technology) services to law firms anywhere in the country. Today, we are moving folks to the cloud, using a data center in northern Virginia. This means we can now provide IT support nationwide and use remote access to connect to any part of your network that is not housed in the data center. Call us if this is an option you want to explore. With all the law firm data breaches that have been reported in the last several years, our Cybersecurity Department has been hopping, investigating data breaches and assessing and securing law firm networks, including doing penetration testing. We also offer employee training and assistance with developing technology-related policies, including incident response plans. More information about our services may be found on our website, https://senseient.com, or you can call Mike Maschke at (703) 359-0700 for further information. Security assessments should be an annual (at least) exercise for all law firms—and they cost less than you might think. We are happy to give you a flat fee quote.

We are serious about our commitment to the legal profession and proud of our professional giveback through the American Bar Association. If you have a question, we'll do our best to assist. Just email us at sensei@senseient.com. We appreciate all your comments and suggestions, as they help make each subsequent edition of this book better than the one before. Thanks, in advance, for your continuing help!

Introduction

by James A. Calloway, Esq.

"Computers are going to take over certain legal tasks—the practice of law will focus more on advice."

Ricardo Anzaldua, Executive Vice President and General Counsel, MetLife

"So quit worrying about what technology will do to you and your firm. Start thinking instead about what it can do for your clients. Figuring out the second point will, in due course, take care of the first."

Jordan Furlong

"Airlocks will likely record exactly who opens them and when, for example, mapping everyone's location down to precise times of day, even to the exact square feet of space they were standing in at a particular moment. Inhabitants' vital signs, such as elevated heart rates and adrenaline levels, will also likely be recorded by sensors embedded in Martian clothing."

How Will Police Solve Murders on Mars? By Geoff Manaugh, *The Atlantic*, posted September 2018

Solving crimes on another planet or defending those accused of them will likely not be an activity that most reading these words will ever have to undertake.

But it's worthwhile noting that the smart phones we all carry with us today record as much information about our physical activities as any habitat on another planet might, including tracking our location. Devices ranging from the FitBit to the Apple Watch 4 record significant amounts of medical information about the wearer, including when one's heart rate is elevated.

We have already seen an Ohio man charged with arson where a significant piece of the evidence against him was a doctor's examination of the man's pacemaker data, which indicated the defendant's statement that he tossed all of his personal possessions out a window after the fire had started was "highly improbable."

A lawyer's competency today involves understanding "the benefits and risks associated with relevant technology" whether or not your jurisdiction has adopted the comment incorporating those words in its Rules of Professional Conduct or not.

Legions of contract lawyers manually doing document review of materials provided in civil discovery have been replaced by predictive coding (a/k/a Technology Assisted Review) since approximately 2012 or 2013. Artificial intelligence tools are likely to change that process even more in the very near future.

Technology changes in society and law practice sometimes require different ways of thinking. A lawyer hired to represent a client injured in an automobile accident still should docket when the statute of limitation expires and immediately notify the insurance carrier of the claim. But the tech savvy lawyer should think about the possibility that some video surveillance or traffic camera recorded relevant information, and that information may be routinely destroyed within a relatively short period of time.

A family practice lawyer representing a client whose spouse just moved out of the home should now ask about whether they have changed their Wi-Fi password, their email password and their router password. They also should inquire whether there are other devices connected to the home network, which could allow an estranged spouse to spy on the client using a security camera or a PlayStation's camera. There have been reports of angry separated spouses mounting psychological attacks by remote controlling thermostats, doorbells, lights and other home appliances connected to the home Wi-Fi network.

Secure digital client portals to share information were first promoted as an alternative to sending confidential client information through the insecure email system. That's still an important consideration. But we see a future ahead where a small firm lawyer or solo practitioner will want to provide more in the client portal than just the documents they would have normally mailed or emailed to the client. One can anticipate that many resources contained in the client portal will become a valuable part of the overall client experience with downloadable resources, helpful reading materials, and instructive videos provided to the law firm's clients.

The lawyer who obstinately refuses to learn about the technology that impacts their practice, and their clients' matters, is clearly now heading for a listing on the endangered professionals list. But before a lawyer can provide groundbreaking new client services, or improved office efficiency through technology, the lawyer has to have basic reliable tools that they use every day—from computers, scanners and printers that work reliably to software tools that are appropriate to the tasks the lawyer needs to accomplish daily and are secure enough to handle confidential client data.

Many legal technology vendors will happily inform a lawyer of why they need to purchase their particular offering, but objective information unimpaired by the need to make a sale is what a lawyer needs before they can intelligently have discussions with a particular vendor.

The 2019 Solo and Small Firm Legal Technology Guide provides objective information about the products that you need to successfully practice law. At times this book will help you make a final decision when trying to select the best tool among competing products. On other occasions, this book will help with a baseline understanding of what a particular product, or class of products, is supposed to help a lawyer accomplish.

As suggested by Jordan Furlong's quote in the opening section, every lawyer needs to make sure his or her basic operating tools are adequate to the tasks of today. Technology-based services more directly impacting the client are clearly on the horizon—at least for forward thinking firms—in the very near future.

This guide can help the lawyer sort through a sometimes puzzling set of features and terms of measurement like terabytes and kilohertz that were not covered in most basic law school curriculums. The expertise of the authors building on their years of experience producing previous editions of this book make this publication an extraordinary value for the solo or small firm lawyer.

CHAPTER ONE

Computers

No decision is as critical to lawyers as deciding which computers/laptops to buy. There are so many choices that lawyers are confounded by the decision-making process. We hope our recommended choices below make the process much easier!

Desktop Computers

Personal Computers (PCs)

The Dell OptiPlex line of computers continues to offer the perfect combination of performance and business-grade hardware at just the right price. All Dell computers can be purchased with a three, four, or five-year warranty and offer a large selection of available options for protecting your investment. They offer both hardware and software warranty protection of varying levels, along with same-day or next-business-day response for the replacement of failed computer hardware or software.

We strongly recommend the purchase of at least a three-year warranty—the typical average life span of a business computer system—with any new computer. Purchasing software technical support, in our judgment, is generally not worth the additional cost, especially when most firms have an IT provider who is familiar with their software and setup and who can assist when help is needed, rather than having to rely on Dell for assistance.

Dell also offers accidental damage protection for its computer systems, which covers damage caused by spilled liquids, drops, falls, and electrical surges for a period of three to five years, at an additional cost ranging from $90 to $132. This is a requirement for lawyers with laptops and not commonly purchased for desktop computer systems, as they are often stored under or to the side of your desk away from possible spills.

Another option from Dell worth noting is its Keep Your Hard Drive program. Typically, if a hard drive crashes while under warranty, Dell will take the failed hard drive and replace it with a new or refurbished one. Citing privacy concerns—with all the continuing data breaches in the news—Dell now offers its users the ability to keep their hard drives, even in the event a replacement is needed, though at an additional cost. The cost for this option ranges from $13 to $19, depending on the length of the warranty (three to five years), and it is a small price to pay to maintain total control over and responsibility for the sensitive and confidential data on the hard drive.

The following table provides our recommendations for a Dell OptiPlex business-grade computer system with all of the hardware components included.

Windows-Based Desktop Computer

Hardware Component	Recommendation
Computer Model:	Dell OptiPlex 7050 Small Form Factor
Operating System:	Microsoft Windows 10 Professional 64-Bit
Processor:	Intel Core i7-8700 3.2 GHz (6 Cores/12MB/12T/ up to 4.6 GHz/65W)
Memory:	8 GB 2x4 GB 2666MHz DDR4 UDIMM Non-ECC
Video Card:	Intel Integrated Graphics
Hard Drive:	3.5 Inch 500 GB 7200RPM Hard Drive accelerated with M.2 Intel Optane Memory 16 GB
Optical Drive:	8X DVD+/-RW
Network:	Intel Gigabit LAN 10/100/1000 Ethernet
Monitor:	2 x Dell 22 inch Monitor—E2216H
Warranty:	Three-year basic hardware service with three-year onsite/in-home service after remote diagnosis
Other:	No mouse and keyboard required; no out-of-band systems management; eight USB 3.0 ports and two USB 2.0 ports included

The eighth-generation Intel Core i7-8700 processor will provide more than enough power to support both current and future versions of business-grade software throughout the life cycle of the machine. The Intel Core i7 processor has become the standard for business-grade systems. The Intel Core i7 processor has varying levels of clock speeds (how fast a processor can churn through data), with the 3.2 GHz version (up to 4.6 GHz Max Turbo

Frequency) currently in the mid-range of processor clock speeds offered by Dell for this model of computer system. The faster the processor, the higher the premium for having cutting-edge technology. The amount of memory included in this system is enough to support your business applications, handling even "memory hungry" applications with ease. Eight gigabytes (GB) of memory have become the recommended standard for the minimum amount of memory in business-grade computers, given the low cost and high gain in performance for the upgrade.

The video card included in this system provides two display port connections, which allows you to have dual monitors or more, an option we will never go without when purchasing a new computer system. John calls his current setup 2 3/4 monitors since he has two 20-inch widescreen monitors and a 15 1/2-inch display on his laptop. This system was configured with two Dell E2216H monitors, offered at a discounted price when bundled with the computer system at a cost of $129 per monitor.

A hard drive plays an important role in the configuration of your computer system because it is the hardware component where your information (files) is actually stored. In short, the better the hard drive is, the faster your computer can read and write your data. This system comes with a 500 GB hard drive, which will provide enough storage space for the average lawyer user. The included Optane Memory allows for more throughput than older SATA hard drives, drastically increasing the speed in which the operating system loads (computer "boots up"), comparable to the speeds of a solid state hard drive.

When configuring an optical drive for the system, choosing the 8X DVD+/–RW drive will allow you to burn and read data from both CDs and DVDs. The Dell OptiPlex 7060 includes ten USB ports (2.0 and 3.0).

Dell offers its OptiPlex 7060 computers preinstalled with the Windows 10 Professional operating systems.

The three-year onsite parts and labor warranty will cover hardware defects and failures of the computer system for a relatively small cost. The cost of this warranty is built into the cost of the recommended system and should be considered a requirement when purchasing a new computer for your business or firm. Dell provides the consumer with a toll-free phone number to call for technical support, and if any hardware needs to be replaced, Dell will send a support technician to your location to replace the defective part after remote diagnosis. The hardware replacement and labor cost is covered by the warranty, so there should be no additional out-of-pocket costs.

There are some additional pointers to consider when configuring this desktop system. First, most users already have their own wireless keyboard and mouse and don't need another basic USB keyboard and mouse taking up space in the desk drawer. This can be avoided by removing them from the default configuration of this system, and you'll save about $10. For those of you who don't have a wireless keyboard and mouse—you should be looking at upgrading immediately. Our recommendations for a wireless desktop suite can be found in the Computer Peripherals chapter, Chapter 3.

For those users who are looking to purchase a new monitor or two, Dell does offer the ability to bundle monitors when configuring your new computer system. If you need a new monitor or two, it may be a good idea to save a few bucks and bundle them with the purchase of your new computer system. Based on a price comparison, it appears that you save about $50 or more per monitor when selecting them at the time of your computer purchase, and we're always looking for ways to save you money! As of this writing, one of the options for monitors is $100 less than Dell's online retail price when bundled—talk about hidden savings!

Keep in mind that, on average, the expected life cycle of a new business computer system is around three years, which is covered by the three-year warranty you purchased. The recommended Dell OptiPlex 7060 Small Form Factor computer with dual monitors can be configured and purchased from Dell's website starting at around $1,400. Remember, you always have the option to extend the warranty for another two years after the initial three-year term if the equipment is still performing satisfactorily and you aren't itching for an upgrade. We know that solo/small firm lawyers often opt to swap out their computer after three years, especially if it seems slower over time, and don't want to pay for a five year warranty that they might not need. Others know that they will keep their machines for five years and want to pay everything at once and up front. That decision is yours.

Remember that the "sweet spot" in buying computers changes regularly. Our specs will get you close, but they will shift slightly during the lifespan of this publication. You can receive a courtesy copy of our current specs (for workstations, laptops, and servers—PC or Mac) by emailing sensei@senseient.com and simply making a request. We are generally able to get our current specs to you within one business day during the workweek. We are happy to report that many, many readers are taking advantage of this offer, so don't be shy. We are always pleased to help.

Apple Computers (Macs)

In the past, Apple computers (Macs) were used primarily by businesses with a need for multimedia functions, such as video editing and graphic design—both areas in which Apple systems have always excelled. Usually, Apple's appearance in an office environment was the result of someone having a personal preference for the Macintosh operating system over the Windows-based system.

Macs are still not as widely used in law offices as Windows-based computers are, but Apple's shift to using Intel-based processors in all of its systems, and the continued popularity of the iPad and iPhone, mean they are chosen more frequently now by solo and small firm lawyers. As a result of the change in processors, Macs can run both the Mac OS X and Windows operating systems on the same computer. In a way, it's like having two systems in one.

A Mac computer can be easily configured to connect to and function on a Windows-based network, including communicating with and authenticating a Windows domain controller, a server computer that responds to security authentication requests (logging in, checking permissions, etc.) within a Windows domain. For those concerned with computer security, Mac systems are perceived to be more secure than their Windows-based counterparts since they are not targeted as often by malware, due to the overall smaller number of Mac users. Some Mac users scoff at the suggestion that their computer should be running some kind of security software for protection. However, they would be wrong; Macs absolutely need security software—and Apple itself has said so for years Remember, the bad guys who write browser exploits (pieces of malware that take advantage of vulnerabilities in internet browsers, such as Firefox) don't care what operating system the computer is running. In fact, security companies consistently warn that malware writers who attack browsers are increasingly becoming the real threat, as vulnerabilities in operating systems are less frequently targeted.

So Apple users, please don't be stubborn—you, too, need virus and malware protection. Apple's continuing release of security patches, even for the latest version of its operating system, is a clear sign of just how much malware developers are targeting this operating system and its applications. For years, we have recommended that security protection suites be installed on all computers, regardless of the operating system.

While they are still not the majority, we are seeing Apple computers make their way into smaller law offices, especially in the solo, stand-alone environment. Since Apple computers use Intel chipsets, users are taking advantage of the opportunity to better integrate their systems with the Windows world. Some users even run Windows on their Mac computers as the primary operating system. Others use Boot Camp, a free utility provided by Apple with each system, to dual-boot between Windows and Mac OS. With Boot Camp, users can install the Microsoft Windows 10 operating system right alongside Apple's OS X on any Intel-based Macintosh computer. Setting up a dual-boot system would be our recommendation, as opposed to running Windows within a virtual machine on a Mac computer.

The most current release of Boot Camp is version 6.1, which added support for Windows 10. Boot Camp 6 includes support for the following features of your Mac in Windows 10: USB 3.0, USB-C, Thunderbolt, built-in Secure Digital or Secure Digital Extended Capacity card slot, USB Apple SuperDrive, and the Apple keyboard, trackpad, and mouse.

The Boot Camp software guides users through the processes of creating a new partition of the local hard drive on which to install the Windows operating system and also provides all of the necessary Windows drivers required for hardware functionality. As an alternative to dual-booting with Boot Camp, some users have even purchased third-party products like Parallels Workstation or downloaded Oracle's VM VirtualBox, which allows them to run Windows, Linux, and other operating systems within the Mac OS itself. Virtual machine (VM) software is described in more detail in the Servers and Server Operating Systems chapters of this book, Chapters 6 and 7.

The iMac desktop systems combine performance and ergonomics by putting the hardware components that make up the system in the same casing as the monitor, eliminating the need for separate components like a tower unit sitting underneath your desk. As a result, the space-saving design allows you to free up both desk and floor space without giving up performance. The following table provides our recommendations for an iMac business-grade desktop system with all of the hardware components outlined.

Macintosh-Based Desktop Computer

Hardware Component	Recommendation
Computer Model:	21.5-inch iMac
Operating System:	MacOS Mojave version 10.14
Processor:	Intel Core i5 Quad-Core 3.0 GHz (Turbo Boost up to 3.5 GHz)
Memory:	8 GB 2400MHz DDR4

Video Card:	Radeon Pro 555 with 2 GB of VRAM, supporting Retina 4K
Hard Drive:	1 TB (5400-rpm) SATA Hard Drive
CD/DVD-ROM:	8X SuperDrive (DVD+R DL/DVD±RW/CD-RW)
Network:	10/100/1000BASE-T Gigabit Ethernet Port, 802.11 ac WI-FI wireless networking (802.11 a/b/g/n compatible), Bluetooth 4.2
Warranty:	Three-year AppleCare Protection Plan for iMacs
Other:	FaceTime HD Camera, built-in 21.5-inch monitor and stereo speakers, microphone, two Thunderbolt 3 ports, four USB 3 ports, Native DisplayPort output over USB-C, Apple wireless keyboard and Magic Mouse 2, SDXC card slot, and Kensington lock slot

The 21.5-inch iMac comes with an Intel Core i5 quad-core 3.0 GHz processor, 8 GB of memory and the latest MacOS Mojave v10.14 operating system. The 1 TB 5400RPM SATA hard drive comes standard and provides more than enough storage space and hard drive performance for the average lawyer. However, if you feel that you need additional storage space or performance speed, the hard drive can be configured with 256 GB of flash storage or Apple's 1 TB Fusion Drive—a combination flash storage and regular hard drive. The flash storage media will contain the files necessary to boot and load the operating system, dramatically increasing the speed with which the computer system starts up.

The standard Ethernet adapter and 802.11 ac Wi-Fi wireless networking adapter will allow your computer to connect to the business network, whether over a wired network or wireless, even if it's Windows-based. The AirPort wireless adapter is also backward compatible with 802.11a/b/g/n wireless networks.

The other standard hardware included with the iMac is the built-in FaceTime HD camera, stereo speakers, 21.5-inch LED-backlit display with intrusion prevention system (IPS) technology, four USB 3.0 ports, two Thunderbolt 3 ports, and one SDXC memory card slot. This system also includes one Mini DisplayPort, which allows users to add a second external monitor to their computer system, and the standard Apple wireless keyboard and Magic Mouse 2. The 21.5-inch iMac computer weighs 12.5 pounds and has a depth of about 7 inches, so finding room on your desk for one of these systems is very easy.

Apple's standard warranty with a new iMac provides you with 90 days of telephone support and a one year limited warranty. We recommend that you upgrade the warranty to the extended AppleCare Protection Plan for iMac, which provides you with telephone and service support for three years. The cost to extend the warranty plan is $169 and is well worth it. The 21.5-inch iMac computer can be purchased from Apple's webstore starting at $1,299.

Laptops

Personal Computers (PCs)

The Dell Latitude line of laptop computers continues to combine performance and mobility in a laptop system that remains at the top of its class. These business-grade laptops are thin and extremely light, weighing less than 4.5 pounds. They are a perfect fit for the mobile lawyer and provide an ideal mobile computing solution. The following table provides our recommendations for a Dell Latitude businessgrade laptop with all of the hardware components included.

Windows-Based Laptop Computer

Hardware Component	Recommendation
Computer Model:	Dell Latitude 7490
Processor:	8th Gen Intel Core i7-8650U 1.9 GHz Processor (Quad-Core, 8M Cache, 15W, vPro)
Operating System:	Microsoft Windows 10 Professional 64-bit
Memory:	8 GB 2400MHz DDR4
Video Card:	Intel Integrated with Chipset
Hard Drive:	M.2 128 GB SATA Class 20 Solid State Hard Drive
CD/DVD-ROM:	None
Network:	10/100/1000 Mbps Ethernet adapter, Intel Dual-Band Wireless-AC 8265 Wi-Fi + BT 4.2 Wireless Driver
Warranty:	Three-year basic hardware service with three-year next-business-day limited on-site service after remote diagnosis
Other:	14-Inch HD AntiGlare Screen, 65W AC power adapter, 60 WHr primary battery with ExpressCharge, weight starting at 3.11 lbs., three USB 3.0 ports, USB Type-C port, HDMI, memory card reader, camera and microphone, SmartCard Reader and Touch Fingerprint Reader

The Dell Latitude E7490 comes with an eighth-generation Intel Core i7-8650U 1.9 GHz processor and 8 GB of memory, which should be sufficient to run all of the business applications of a mobile lawyer. The system also comes preinstalled with Microsoft Windows 10 Professional.

The system's fingerprint reader provides the level of security needed to protect your personal files and confidential data. When it's enabled, you can restrict user logon access to either the biometric access or to a user name and password. A fingerprint reader keeps data on the hard drive secure through encryption, with the hardware requiring successful authentication before the data contents can be decrypted. Enabling a start-up or hard drive password in the system's BIOS is a great way to add an extra layer of protection to your system, as is encrypting the hard drive with full-disk encryption.

The integrated graphics supply crisp, clear graphics to the 14-inch wide LCD display. The 128 GB hard drive provides more than enough storage space for the mobile user, with a hard drive speed that will supply faster drive performance. There is no internal optical drive (CD/DVD drive) included with this model, so if you need to read optical discs, you will need to look at external solutions. Frankly, optical drives in laptops are a thing of the past. Flash drives have replaced external file transfers, and more and more software applications are delivered via download.

The Ethernet adapter will allow you to connect your laptop to your network when you're in the office, and the wireless network adapter will allow you to stay connected when on the move. The Intel wireless adapter provides connectivity to all wireless networks, supporting dual-band operation (2.4 and 5 GHz) with data rates up to 300 megabits per second (Mbps). The four-cell battery is an upgrade that will supply the laptop with power longer than the standard three-cell battery and should charge faster as well with the ExpressCharge feature. Finally, the integrated HD video webcam and digital microphone are great for video conferences or recording audio, such as podcasts.

The three-year, next-business day onsite parts and labor warranty is the same warranty described in the Desktop Computers section. The Dell Latitude 7490 can be purchased from Dell's website starting at around $1,659.

If you are particularly clumsy or accident-prone, you may want to consider adding the Accidental Damage Service to your purchase. This plan covers any damage to the laptop, including such things as liquid spills (one client has used this plan multiple times to cover the unwelcome effects of spilling red wine), surges, and dropping the device. It does not cover intentional damage, theft, or normal wear and tear. For the additional $90 to $132, depending on the length of the warranty (three to five-year options), you will have peace of mind when you set your coffee cup (or wine glass) on the keyboard, both of which are ill-advised actions!

Apple Computers (Macs)

The Apple MacBook Pro is perfect for the mobile lawyer who requires a powerful notebook in a compact and lightweight design. The MacBook Pro laptop comes standard with a widescreen Retina display, built-in FaceTime HD camera, wireless network adapter, and much more. The MacBook Pro laptop is available with 13- or 15-inch screens. Both the 13- and 15-inch MacBook Pros come standard with the Retina display. The MacBook Pro is available in both Silver and Space Gray with glass LED-backlit display with IPS technology. The MacBook Pro can be fully integrated into any Windows-based network without too much overhead and configuration. The following table provides our recommendations for an Apple MacBook Pro business-grade laptop with all of the hardware components included.

Macintosh-Based Laptop Computer

Hardware Component	Recommendation
Computer Model:	15-Inch MacBook Pro
Operating System:	MacOS Mojave version 10.14
Processor:	2.2 GHz 6-core intel Core i7, Turbo Boost up to 4.1 GHz, with 9MB shared L3 Cache
Memory:	16 GB 2400MHz DDR4
Video Card:	Radeon Pro 555 with 4 GB of GDDR5 memory
Hard Drive:	256 GB Solid State Hard Drive
CD/DVD-ROM:	None
Network:	802.11ac Wi-Fi wireless networking (802.11 a/b/g/n compatible), Bluetooth 5.0
Warranty:	Three-year AppleCare Protection Plan
Other:	FaceTime HD Camera, built-in 15.4-inch LED—backlit display with IPS technology, stereo speakers, four Thunderbolt 3 ports (USB-C), and display port, Touch Bar with integrated Touch ID sensor

The base 15-inch MacBook Pro laptop comes with 16 GB of memory and the MacOS Mojave v10.14 operating system. The Radeon Pro 555 video card provides perfect high resolution to the 15.4 inch-wide Retina LED display, with a maximum resolution of 2880 × 1800 pixels. The 256 GB Solid State Drive provides enough space to store all of your documents, pictures, and music. The laptop no longer comes with an internal optical drive, so if you need to be able to read and burn optical discs, you will need to look at external solutions. The built-in 802.11ac Wi-Fi wireless networking adapter will keep you connected on the road, and it supports the 802.11n standard. The adapter is also backward compatible with 802.11a/b/g wireless networks. The aluminum body MacBook is very light, weighing just barely over 4 pounds. If you need more processing power, this model can be upgraded with an Intel i7 2.6 GHz six-core processor—for a pretty penny!

The Force Touch trackpad gives you precise cursor control and supports two-finger scrolling, tap, double-tap, and drag capabilities. It also now supports pressure-sensing capabilities. If you have been a lifelong Windows user, be forewarned: There is no right-click button on the trackpad. To right-click on a Mac, you must hold down the Control key while clicking. A tip for former Windows users: Instead of holding down the Control key to initiate a right-click, you can tap the trackpad with two fingers—you just have to enable the option within the Keyboard & Mouse settings. The new integrated Touch Bar replaces the function keys that used to appear at the top of the keyboard, providing users with more versatile functions that change with what you're doing on the screen. Apple has also included Touch ID, enabling instant access to logins and fast, secure online purchases with Apple Pay.

The Thunderbolt 3 charger allows users to charge and provide power from any of the four ports, and since Thunderbolt 3 is reversible, no matter how users plug in the adapter, it's always the right way!

The sleek and elegant design of the MacBook Pro is what sets it apart from the competition. The design and celebrated ease of use makes the MacBook Pro a smart choice when purchasing a laptop for yourself or your firm. The MacBook Pro configured above can be purchased from Apple's webstore for $2,399.

Netbooks/Ultrabooks

Netbooks and ultrabooks continue to be very popular among mobile users, including lawyers. Essentially, these devices are highly portable mini-laptops. They are much smaller, cheaper, and lighter than most traditional laptops. As with the other computer recommendations, it is impossible to mention all of the available manufacturers and models of ultrabooks and netbooks.

More recently, netbooks have all but disappeared thanks to the class of laptops called ultrabooks. Ultrabooks, which are becoming increasingly popular, are paper-thin laptops (nearly weightless compared to a traditional laptop). Ultrabooks have more robust hardware specifications than netbooks, but they also command a premium price.

Apple released the MacBook Air, an ultrabook considered the first of its class, long before PC manufacturers released the first competitor. Much as the iPad has dominated Android-based tablets, in part because it was first to the market, the MacBook Air continues to be an extremely popular alternative to the regular laptop for a mobile user.

The MacBook Air is offered in two 13-inch models (with or without Retina display), with configurable internal flash storage capacity available from 128 to 512 GB. The 1.8 GHz Dual Core Intel Core i5 processor (Turbo Boost up to 2.9 GHz) is more than capable of handling web browsing and document editing, but not a lot more than that, which is perfect for the mobile lawyer. The processor can be upgraded to a 2.2 GHz dual-core Intel Core i7. The MacBook Air now comes standard with 8 GB of memory and two USB 3 ports. The battery of the MacBook Air will last up to 12 hours when surfing the web.

If you were to hold the MacBook Air, weighing just 2.96 pounds, you'd never go back to using a standard laptop. The MacBook Air is available for purchase on Apple's website starting at $999.

Tablets

Microsoft Surface Pro

Business-grade tablets, those that can truly replace a laptop, are quickly becoming the next big thing in solo and small firm technology. For the last several years, Sharon and John have been bombarded with questions on this very topic at many of the presentations that they give throughout the country—is there a tablet that can actually replace my laptop, while maintaining all of the functionality?

The answer is, yes there is. You can now leave your 4.5 pound laptop and clunky travel bag at home when you need to hit the road.

The Microsoft Surface Pro is truly a laptop replacement unlike the Apple iPad, which we discuss below. For those users that want an even smaller device, Microsoft has released the Surface Go with a 10-inch screen. The Surface Pro tablet boasts a 12.3-inch PixelSense touchscreen display with a resolution of 2736 × 1824. The eighth-generation Intel Core processor (i5, i7) is the same processor that you will find in your laptop computer system, and it provides this tablet with more than enough horsepower to run your business applications smoothly. The tablet comes preloaded with Microsoft Windows 10, which means that you can load and run any of your necessary business software—allowing you to get the same functionality out of this device as you can out of your laptop—at just a fraction of the weight!

The device can be configured with 8 or 16 GB of memory and anywhere from 128 GB to 1TB of storage space. For network connectivity, this device comes with a 802.11ac wireless adapter supporting 802.11a/b/g/n and Bluetooth 4.1 wireless technology. It has both a front and rear-facing camera, as well as a stereo microphone perfect for videoconferencing. We would recommend that you give serious consideration to the 16 GB memory, 512 GB storage, i7 unit priced at $1,899.

The Microsoft Surface Pro tablet can be purchased online from Microsoft's webstore (www.microsoft.com) or from your local electronics retailer starting at $799.

Apple iPad Pro

Year after year, Apple continues to provide more hype and enthusiasm about the next version of the iPad, and it has continued to find ways to improve this device.

In September 2015, Apple first released the iPad Pro and has since then continued to update this model line every year. This behemoth device, larger than any previously released iPad by almost 3 inches, is targeted toward businesses, with its sights set directly on the Surface Pro market share. We have yet to see a large portion of the business market share adopt iPad Pros, with more attorneys and technical staff preferring the Microsoft Surface Pro for a number of reasons.

This device comes with either an 11- or 12.9-inch Liquid Retina display and nearly double the CPU performance of the iPad Air 2. This device is powered by the A12X, Bionic chip with 64-bit architecture. The 12.9-inch LED-backlit wide-screen multi-touch display boasts a resolution of 2732 × 2048. The refined multi-touch technology adds another dimension to the user experience. The camera has been kept the same at 12 MP (megapixels) and can record 4K HD video at 30 frames per second. This device also contains four speakers.

The iPad Pro comes with a built-in Wi-Fi network card with two antennas supporting the 802.11ac protocol, enabling the device to connect to wireless networks, and the 4G model comes with a broadband AirCard and GPS locator. The device also includes Bluetooth 5.0 capability and a 29.37 watt-hour (or 36.71 watt-hour) battery lasting up to ten hours, even when continually surfing the internet. This version of the iPad is available with 64, 256, 512 GB or 1 TB of internal memory at a starting cost of $799.

Since the release of the iPad Pro, Apple has released the next version of its iOS software, version 12, which comes preinstalled on all new iPad devices. Apple is already pushing iOS version 12 on its website, touting new features such as increased performance, opening up the camera, keyboard display, and app launch under heavy workload. iOS 12 also allows FaceTime calls to include up to 32 people at one time, with the tile of the person speaking getting larger so that the user can track the conversation. There are a few new augmented reality experiences that are included with the new iOS version, which have been available in apps like Snapchat for several years now. One of the biggest new features that we are looking forward to is the inclusion of Screen Time. With the increasing number of users addicted to and glued to their mobile devices all day long, along with the health and well-being of attorneys a focus of CLEs throughout the country, being aware of how much you actually use your device each day is very informative—and frightening! Screen Time is also geared towards parents who want to limit or set restrictions on how much their children can use the mobile device each day. The Screen Time app is very granular with restrictions being able to be set up on most apps, with daily and weekly usage reports able to be viewed and emailed. If anyone needs a jump-start to put down their device every once in a while, nothing is better than actual data to get you started!

In our opinion, the last revolutionary change to the iOS software was iOS 5, when Apple introduced its iCloud service. The iCloud service allows users to synchronize their music, photos, apps, documents, bookmarks, calendar, contacts, email, and other data between multiple iOS devices. As a cloud service, Apple will actually store this data for you in an online account associated with your Apple ID. As with many Apple products, we have determined there are a number of security and privacy concerns with using this service. If you don't believe us, just read the terms of service—we did, and we will not use this service for anything business related. If you have enabled iCloud, be careful with what information you choose to synchronize with

Apple. Many celebrities now understand that after the Celebgate debacle of 2014, when naked photos of them flooded the internet. That's all we will say. We only have the Find My iPad feature configured in iCloud so that we can locate the device if lost. Unfortunately, that also means Apple knows where our iPad is at all times. Unlike the iPhone, Apple has the ability to decrypt the data stored in iCloud, which is another reason to be wary of storing data in iCloud. If you must use the iCloud service, even if only for personal use, we recommend implementing two-factor authentication with this service to provide an extra layer of protection against unauthorized access to your account.

Today, lawyers frequently use the iPad for court or meetings, rather than lugging around a laptop. Originally thought to compete against e-book devices such as the Kindle and Nook, the iPad has actually established a new class of devices that compete against smartphones, netbooks, smaller laptops, and ultrabooks. Lawyers are drawn to the functionality and portability of the device, and like the consistency of using Apple products at work if they do so at home.

CHAPTER TWO

Computer Operating Systems

Older versions of the Microsoft Windows operating system (Windows 7 and older) are not addressed in this book, mainly because most of the versions are no longer relevant and the majority (7 is the exception) are no longer supported by Microsoft, which means they should not be used by businesses or individuals due to the insecurity of these operating systems. Windows 7 has entered the "Extended Support" phase that lasts through January 14, 2020, but is not an operating system that we recommend users or firms continue to use. More on that later.

Every now and then, we still come across law firms that are using computers running Microsoft Windows XP. Please note that Microsoft no longer supports this operating system and its use should immediately cease. Legal ethicists regard its continued use as an ethical violation since it is no longer receiving security updates and places confidential client data at risk. Computers running Microsoft Windows XP should be decommissioned and replaced as soon as possible.

Microsoft has stated that Windows 7 "does not meet the requirements of modern technology, nor the high security requirements of IT departments," as Microsoft continues to push end users and businesses to upgrade systems to the Windows 10 operating system. It is our recommendation that all computers should be upgraded to Windows 10 as soon as possible or if more cost effective, outdated systems should be replaced. Independent experts have confirmed that Windows 7 genuinely cannot be secured and confirmed Microsoft's assertions that Windows 10 is so good that it has been found to stop "zero-day" exploits (brand new malware or other forms of cyberattacks).

Microsoft Windows 8

Windows 8 is the successor to Windows 7 and became available to consumers in early fall of 2012. The Windows 8 user interface is built based on the Metro design language, featuring a new start screen, Internet Explorer 10, support for USB 3.0, and a new Windows Defender. Windows 8 also added support for UEFI SecureBoot, which is a feature used to prevent unauthorized firmware, operating systems, or drivers from running at boot time.

There was much controversy over the Metro look, replacing the all-too-familiar Windows Start button. The Metro UI environment is tile-based, similar to the Start screen seen on the Windows Phone operating system. The Start button had originally been removed from the taskbar, but was later reinstated with the update, Windows 8.1, released in October 2013.

Windows 8 is available in four editions, three of which are focused on business-grade computers: Windows 8, Windows 8 Pro, and Windows 8 Enterprise. The Windows RT edition is built to run solely on tablet hardware.

Windows 8 has been available for a several years now and is heading toward a fate similar to Windows Vista. The adoption of this operating system by businesses never took off, and even that may be a generous description. We never upgraded our own computer systems to Windows 8 and went straight from Windows 7 to Windows 10. We have been purchasing new computers for our clients with Windows 10 installed for a few years now.

Microsoft Windows 10

Windows 10, the latest operating system from Microsoft, is the successor to Windows 8 and was released to the public on July 29, 2015. Microsoft used to offer a free upgrade path to Windows 10 for those computers running Windows 7 Service Pack 1 or Windows 8.1, but that offer has come and gone. For users wanting to upgrade, Microsoft sells Windows 10 Pro licenses for $199 but you may find a copy sold for less by other retailers.

Microsoft introduced a universal application architecture across all Microsoft product families including computers, tablets, smartphones, and Xbox One, allowing for applications to be designed and run across all of the devices—similar to the iOS environment. One of the main features that was included was an updated Start Menu (combination of Windows 7 and 8), a new web browser named Microsoft Edge, and integrated support for fingerprint and facial recognition logins. Microsoft's Edge browser is now the default browser in Windows 10 and has adopted the HTML5 specification, dropping much of the support for legacy Internet Explorer releases (meaning websites developed for IE6 or IE7 won't render in this new browser).

Also new to this operating system is the inability for users to be able to selectively install Windows updates. Microsoft now installs all Windows updates automatically. The release of this software has been positively received by the public, but one of the initial criticisms, and a valid one, involves privacy concerns. By default, the system transmits user data to Microsoft and/or its partners, a troubling development. For now, it's not easy to restrict what Windows collects. The data can be restricted—it's easier if users don't use the Express Settings during setup, but rather select the "custom install" to turn off some of the data collecting options. As an alternative, you can try one of the free tools to change the settings in a more user-friendly interface (bgr.com/2015/08/14/windows-10-spying-prevention-privacy-tools/). Subsequent releases of Windows 10 have continued to improve upon the privacy settings. You can now totally disable all Windows Telemetry data in Windows 10. Just do a Google search for "windows 10 telemetry data" to get advice on how and what data collection to disable.

Windows 10 Pro and Enterprise come with Microsoft's BitLocker encryption software at no additional cost. We strongly recommend that users encrypt all data on portable systems including laptops and tablets running Windows 10. Please note that desktop computers should be encrypted as well.

Windows 10 is the ONLY operating system of choice when purchasing a new computer system or upgrading an existing one. Windows 7 should no longer be used.

MacOS Mojave Version 10.14 Operating System

Released to the public in September 2018, MacOS Mojave is the latest major release of Apple's Mac operating system for desktops and servers. This operating system brings several iOS apps to the desktop, including Apple News, Voice Memos, Home and is the final version of MacOS to support 32-bit apps. Third-party iOS developers will be able to move over their apps sometime in 2019. Some of the new security features include the enhancements to Safari's tracking prevention feature, which now blocks social media buttons and widgets from tracking users without permission. It will also flag users when the browser detects reused passwords so that users can change them. There are also new data protections that require apps get user permissions before accessing the camera or microphone. Like previous versions, it also has built-in encryption (File Vault 2), crash-safe protections and a simplified data backup on the go. Like its Windows counterpart, we strongly recommend that users encrypt all data on portable systems including laptops, tablets, and desktops.

Apple is also claiming that the new operating system contains massive increases in graphics speed, thanks to the Metal 2 technology built into the operating system that allows apps to utilize the full power of the Graphics Processor Unit. This inclusion also adds capabilities like machine learning and virtual reality. Finally, with this latest release, Apple has updated and enhanced most of the default apps like Photos, Safari, and the Messages app.

Users who have switched on automatic downloads and have enough storage on their Macs will automatically be prompted to get the latest version of MacOS—it will not install without permission. Like previous releases of Mac operating systems, this update is free and should be installed when prompted.

CHAPTER THREE

Computer Peripherals

If you thought purchasing the right computer and monitor was tough, wait until you realize how many options there are when it comes to selecting computer peripherals. Having the right peripherals can make your computing faster, more comfortable, and a better overall, productive experience. Wireless devices have brought peripherals into a new dimension, getting rid of that Gordian knot mess of wires that we all used to struggle to untangle. The following sections provide our recommendations for portable mice, wireless desktops (keyboards and mouse), external storage devices, and speakers. As always, bear in mind that there is a universe of choices. These are our top picks.

Portable Mouse

For portability, those users who travel with laptops and want a nifty little wireless travel mouse should consider the excellent Microsoft Wireless Mobile Mouse 4000. Using 2.4 GHz wireless technology, this mouse connects to your computer with a reliable connection range of up to 30 feet. The nano transceiver that you plug into the USB port of your computer has a slot inside the mouse to store it when on the go. This mouse uses Microsoft's BlueTrack technology to smoothly track the mouse movements on virtually any surface, even on your living room carpet. This notebook mouse also includes the standard back button and scroll wheel, in an ergonomic design that we've all become accustomed to. If you are concerned about the current battery life, the mouse includes an indicator light that will glow red when the batteries need to be replaced—and it only requires a single AA battery, which is included. The battery should last ten months or more before needing replacement. Of course, you do need to look at the light periodically so that you don't end up with a dead mouse and have to scramble for a new battery. This mouse is compatible with both Windows and Mac computers, including the Windows 10 operating system, and can be purchased online from Microsoft's website for $34.95. We've actually seen this mouse recently at a local department/electronics warehouse for less than half the online cost—just an FYI.

Wireless Keyboards

Over the past decade or so, wireless keyboards have become extremely popular—so popular that it's almost impossible to find a USB keyboard and mouse. In fact, it's been so many years since we purchased a stand-alone mouse or keyboard that we no longer provide recommendations for these devices. We recommend the purchase of a wireless keyboard set instead. A wireless keyboard set is a keyboard and mouse combination that connects to your computer using radiofrequency (RF) technology. The keyboard and mouse are powered with standard or rechargeable batteries and transmit their signals to a desktop receiver that is connected to the computer. It requires very little setup to install, and it eliminates the need for cables, which have plagued computer users since the first PC came into existence.

Our recommendation when purchasing a wireless keyboard set is the Logitech Wireless Wave Combo MK550. This wireless keyboard comes with a wave-shaped key design that provides superior comfort with full-size and full-travel keys designed for quiet operation. The slight regular curve of the keyboard features consistently sized keys, which lets you type with confidence and ease. The keyboard uses the standard QWERTY layout, so you don't have to relearn how to type, as you do with some of the other curved keyboards. The height of the keyboard is adjustable, with three options for leg height, allowing you to choose the position that's most comfortable for you. The keyboard comes with a cushioned, contoured palm rest to provide comfort to your wrists. The keyboard uses 128-bit AES encryption to secure data as it's transmitted from the keyboard, and both the keyboard and mouse use the 2.4 GHz wireless spectrum to connect to the receiver. Logitech claims that the keyboard can operate up to three years before the batteries need to be replaced, and if true, the batteries should last the expected lifetime of the keyboard. The package includes four AA batteries, with the keyboard and mouse each requiring two.

Logitech's wireless laser mouse M510, which is part of the MK550 combination, should operate for up to two years before the batteries will need to be replaced. The laser mouse uses a small infrared laser instead of an LED sensor, which increases the resolution and sensitivity of the mouse. The laser mouse keeps your hands pain-free with the integration of contoured sides and soft rubber grips. The Logitech Wireless Wave Combo includes a three-year limited hardware warranty. This wireless keyboard combo is compatible with Windows 10. The Logitech Wireless Wave Combo MK550 can be purchased for under $50 from your local electronics retailer or online at www.logitech.com.

External Storage Devices

External storage devices are pieces of hardware that connect to your computer using USB, FireWire, eSATA, or some other type of interface and are used to store electronic data. These devices come in all sizes, shapes, colors, and volumes of storage space. They have replaced the CD-ROM, DVD, and backup tapes as the leading means to store electronic data because of their portability, low cost, and vast amount of storage space. You should consider some type of secure authentication or encryption when using external storage, especially if confidential client information is backed up or stored on these devices. Most products now come with built-in hardware or software encryption that can be enabled at no additional cost. Just be sure to remember your passphrase, because if you forget it, there's no way to recover your data.

External Hard Drives

External hard drives are great devices for storing media such as videos and pictures and for backing up the data from the internal hard drive of your computer. These devices are very easy to install and use, and are relatively inexpensive. Most external hard drives are plug-and-play devices, which means you simply have to plug them into your computer to use them—and nothing else is required! The operating system automatically loads the drivers necessary for these devices to work, and they are a very good, inexpensive backup solution. Lawyers who are otherwise technically challenged seem to do well with this form of backup, which can really be reduced to the push of a button or an automated method that so many lawyers seem to prefer—set it and forget it, just like Ron Popeil would extol to his audiences when demonstrating his Showtime Rotisserie.

The Seagate Backup Plus Hub is the external hard drive that we recommend for all lawyers and users. The Backup Plus Hub comes with available capacities of 4, 6, 8 and 10 TB of storage space. These capacities allow you to select the amount of storage space that best meets your requirements and may provide enough storage capacity to contain backups from more than one computer system. All Backup Plus Hub drives include two integrated USB 3.0 ports on the front of the devices, so that you can back up your files while connecting to and recharging your tablet, smartphone, or camera—even if your computer is powered off. The Backup Plus Hub comes with backup software that can be used to automatically back up your data to the device, and it is Windows 10 compatible. You can now even use the Seagate Mobile Backup app to easily back up photos and videos on the go directly from your mobile device to the Backup Plus Hub.

All of the available models should provide enough storage space to back up all of the data required by most lawyers. If you're looking to back up multiple computers and/or a server, then you probably will need to purchase one of the larger-sized drives—and make sure that you purchase more than one. We recommend that if you're using this external hard drive to back up your company data and files, then you should rotate drives on a weekly or more frequent basis—keeping one onsite and the other one offsite. This will allow your firm to recover its information in the event of a disaster such as a fire in the office. With the prevalence of ransomware infections, we recommend disconnecting the drive when it is not being used—and keeping an encrypted copy "in the cloud." That way if your computer gets infected with ransomware such as WannaCry, your data won't get encrypted and you will have backups that can be used to restore your information.

These devices connect to your computer through the USB 3.0 interface (backward compatible with USB 2.0) and can be placed flat or on their side. The drive is whisper quiet and relatively small in size, so it can sit on your desk or on top of your computer without taking away valuable space. Compatible with both Windows and Mac computers, the drive includes a new technology file system (NTFS) driver for Macs that will allow interoperability between systems without the need to reformat the drive. The Backup Plus Desktop Drive can be purchased online at www.seagate.com for between $129 and $359, depending on the storage capacity, and it comes with a two-year standard warranty.

Flash Drives

USB flash drives (thumb drives) are small, portable storage devices that use flash memory to store electronic data. Currently, they are offered with storage volume sizes ranging from 16 GB to 1 TB. For the most part, USB flash drives with capacities of 8 GB and smaller have been discontinued—in fact, our local computer supply store has all but gotten rid of USB flash drives less than 16 GB! USB flash drives offer many advantages over other portable storage devices, such as the floppy disk, CD-ROM, and DVD. In particular, they are smaller, are more durable, are faster, and can hold more data. Unfortunately, these devices also pose a great security risk for small businesses and law firms because their small size makes them absurdly easy to lose. This risk can be minimized, however, by using the SanDisk Ultra USB 3.0 flash drive, which comes standard with 128-bit AES encryption to keep data secure.

This model is available with 16, 32, 64, 128, or 256 GB of storage space for your files. Using the SanDisk SecureAccess software, a user can protect access to private files with password protection and encryption. The software creates a file vault (protected folder) on the USB drive, creating a secure storage location for the user to place and keep all sensitive and confidential data. The SanDisk SecureAccess software is compatible with the Windows 10 and Mac OS X v.10.6+ operating systems, although Mac users will have to download the supporting software from the App Store.

The SanDisk Ultra USB flash drives can be purchased online at https://www.sandisk.com for between $8 and $62, depending on the storage capacity, and all come with a five-year limited warranty. Some of the other online retailers that SanDisk may refer you to for purchasing its products may have lower retail pricing than SanDisk—so check carefully.

For those users who require top-of-the-line security, look no further than the IronKey Basic S1000 USB device, which comes in 4, 8, 16, 32, 64, and 128 GB versions. The S1000 version can read data at speeds up to 320 Mbps, about 10 times faster than the S250 version. This flash drive is also fast, featuring transfer speeds of up to 350 Mbps.

This USB device is designed for the needs of sensitive military, government, and enterprise networks and includes XTS-AES 256-bit hardware encryption that has been validated to meet government Federal Information Processing Standard (FIPS) requirements, specifically FIPS 140-2 Level 3. The security features require no software or drivers to install, with all the security being handled by the device hardware, and the features are always on. The device requires that a user authenticate with a password before encryption keys are enabled and data can be accessed.

This device is even waterproof! As these devices tend to be inadvertently placed in washing machines while in the pocket of your pants, this is an excellent feature, though we've not yet put it to the test. This device has a self-destruct mechanism (think *Mission: Impossible* without the smoke) that will wipe (i.e., permanently and irretrievably remove) the data contents if a user or thief tries to break into the IronKey and enters ten incorrect passwords. The IronKey Basic S1000 USB can be purchased online from Kingston's website (www.kingston.com) for $139 to $849, depending on the storage capacity.

Another great choice for an encrypted USB flash drive is the Kingston DataTraveler 4000 G2, offered with storage capacity ranging from 4 to 64 GB. This affordable solution provides business-grade security, USB 3.0 connectivity and FIPS 140-2 Level 3 certification, for those firms (or their clients) that require certified compliance requirements for their hardware. This USB flash drive uses 256-bit AES hardware-based encryption to protect data stored on the drive, and after ten intrusion attempts (incorrect password guesses) the device will lock and reformat itself, rending all of the previously existing data unrecoverable. This device can be purchased online from Kingston's website (www.kingston.com) starting at $79.00 for the 4 GB model.

Speakers

Lawyers (and their staff) often tell us that the most important peripheral device they need for their computer is a pair of speakers. They like to be able to listen to music while they work and are adamant about fidelity. Reasonable quality desktop speakers can be purchased, without breaking the bank, to provide the user with a clear, true sound. Logitech, a leading provider of speaker systems for computers, makes the Z213 Compact 2.1 Speaker System. They offer 2.1 stereo sound with a subwoofer, providing enhanced bass, and the speakers come in a slim, stylish profile. The speakers have a stereo headphone jack, an auxiliary input where you can connect your iPod or MP3 player, and integrated controls located on a wired remote. They even include a cable management system to help reduce the clutter of wires. These speakers offer quality audio at a reasonable price. The Logitech Multimedia Speakers Z213 can be purchased online for around $30 from www.logitech.com.

If you purchase one of the recommended Dell flat-panel monitors, consider adding a sound bar. The sound bar clips onto the bottom edge of the Dell flat-panel and gets its power from the monitor itself. It provides a clean installation and doesn't take up any additional desk space. The model of the sound bar will vary depending on the Dell monitor that you wish to attach the speakers to, so be sure to check out Dell's website to ensure that you select the appropriate model.

CHAPTER FOUR

Printers

Even in the era of the "paperless" office, most law firms still print many documents on a daily basis, probably more than any other type of business. To say that the practice of law tends to be less than green is a massive understatement—although most firms have implemented a recycling program. In fairness, more and more firms are committing to going paperless, but it has been a long and tortured path. Nonetheless, it is certainly critical to have a good, reliable printer to ensure that your firm is printing quality documents in the quickest time possible. In the following sections, we discuss and recommend printers for stand-alone systems, network systems, and multifunctional printers/copiers.

Stand-Alone Printers

The most basic type of printer is the stand-alone printer, which connects directly to a computer and is not placed on the network. It only has to be capable of handling a single user's print jobs. Even in environments where networked printers are used and recommended, there can be valid reasons to have stand-alone printers—perhaps so the bookkeeper can keep financial records from inadvertently being picked up by someone else. Senior partners may feel their information is so confidential that they want a printer in their office (though their staff often mutter that they are just too lazy to walk down the hall). Many makes and models of stand-alone printers are available to choose from, and each has different performance specifications, features, and available fonts.

The question about whether to use an inkjet printer is dead. No more inkjet. We highly recommend going with a laser printer. Inkjet printers typically result in a higher cost of ownership over the long haul, with ink cartridges printing at a higher cost per page than the average laser printer. There are even studies that show a cost of $3,000–$5,000 per gallon for name-brand ink cartridges. Human blood is cheaper. Laser is better quality and more economical—case closed.

A stand-alone printer can be shared through enabling File and Print Sharing on your local computer, but we strongly counsel against this practice. Enabling this service creates a host of security vulnerabilities that could compromise not only your system but also your entire network, and it causes many management and configuration headaches for the IT administrator.

When discussing printers with our clients, we are frequently asked, "Should I purchase a color or a black-and-white laser printer?" You will pay a slight premium for a color laser printer, and in most instances, it is not worth the cost when purchasing a stand-alone printer. It is usually more cost effective to purchase a color laser printer to be placed on the local computer network and shared so that more than one user can print to it.

The Hewlett-Packard (HP) LaserJet Pro M203dw black-and-white laser printer is the perfect solution for the stand-alone or network (up to five users) printer. The printer has a built-in Ethernet connection, along with USB and wireless support for network connectivity, and prints in duplex (two-sided) mode by default. This printer prints as many as 30 pages per minute, comes standard with a paper input capacity of 250 sheets, and has a recommended monthly volume of up to 2,500 pages but can support a monthly duty cycle of up to 30,000 pages if needed. In general, the monthly duty cycle is the maximum number of pages a device can print in a month where the recommended monthly print volume is the amount to print to keep the device in optimal condition. The printer has a first-page-out speed of 6.6 seconds and supports all the common page types, such as letter, legal, executive, and envelopes. This printer comes standard with 256 MB of memory and can connect to your computer using the USB interface. It should be noted that the printer does come with a USB cable, whereas previous HP models we've recommended have not. For mobile users, this printer is compatible with Apple's AirPrint service, which allows users to print to the device from their iPad, iPhone, or iPod touch—a feature that is quickly becoming a necessity with the increasing number of iPads and iPhones being used in the workplace. Using the HP ePrint app, Android mobile users can print directly from their mobile device as well. Users can also print directly to the printer using Wi-Fi Direct.

This black-and-white printer is great for quick business printing and offers a cost-effective solution for personal printing. The printer is both Mac and Windows compatible, including Windows 10. It also comes standard with a one-year limited warranty. The HP LaserJet Pro M203dw printer can be purchased online for around $199.99 (before discounts) from www.hp.com. At the time of writing, this printer was discounted to a cost of $129.99 on HP's webstore.

If you're looking for tips on how to reduce the frequency with which you have to purchase replacement laser cartridges, there are a few things you can do. First, look into software that automatically removes wasted pages from printing jobs, especially common when printing out content from websites using your internet browser. This printer comes with software called HP Smart Web Printing that you can install on your local computer, which reduces the wasted pages and space when printing from websites. Another great tip is to change the print quality to "Draft" if the document is just going to be discarded shortly after printing and not something official that you're going to submit to court. This alone can save you lots of toner.

Networked Printers

Networked printers provide a printing resource to multiple users and are accessible to users from a central location throughout the local network. This configuration reduces the number of printers that your firm will need to purchase and administer. The administration and security of these printers can be integrated into your network's security infrastructure, such as through Windows Active Directory for a Windows-based network, and networking a printer is much more secure than sharing it through the File and Print Sharing service. You should consider disabling the remote administration function (via a web browser) for the printer. Remote administration typically means that a specialized website is running on the printer. These web services are rarely secure and fairly easy to compromise.

We recommend installing the printer in a central location, which simplifies the management, administration, and security of these devices. Network printers can be shared with the various computers and users that make up your network with very little overhead and effort. Many types of networked printers are available, and depending on your need—low volume, high volume, color—your options will vary. A popular request from many law offices is to have multiple trays for the printer. The capability to have multiple paper types loaded is usually available in the mid-range to higher-end printer models.

Low-Volume Network Printers

Low-volume network printers are designed for workgroups of users having a small to moderate print volume, as high as 5,000 pages per month. These printers are moderately priced and are primarily used to segment printing within offices based on user group or physical location. Network printers have more robust hardware than stand-alone printers to handle multiple jobs from different users at the same time.

The HP LaserJet Pro M402dw black-and-white network-based laser printer is great for a small law firm because it provides users with a highly reliable, cost-effective printer that is capable of handling the expected volume produced by the average small firm. The HP LaserJet Pro M402dw prints as many as 40 pages per minute and has a recommended monthly print volume of up to 4,000 pages. This model also has a monthly duty cycle of up to 80,000 pages. It comes standard with an input capacity of 350 sheets and 128 MB of memory, and it handles all paper sizes. This printer has a first-page-out speed of 6.4 seconds. As an added feature, the printer allows for automatic duplexing for printing double-sided documents.

The printer has an embedded gigabit Ethernet network adapter to attach the printer to your local network and a built-in Wi-Fi 802.11 b/g/n adapter for wireless connectivity. This printer also supports Apple's AirPrint service, allowing users to print directly from their iPad, iPhone, or iPod Touch device or using the HP ePrint app, for those using Android mobile devices. For additional security, this printer can prevent unauthorized access with management features including 802.1x authentication and password protection. This model does come with a USB cable for connecting directly to a USB port.

The memory of this printer is upgradeable, and the printer's drivers are compatible with both Mac and Windows-based systems, including Windows 10. The printer comes with a standard one-year warranty and includes a CD-ROM with the drivers and software necessary to configure the device. The HP LaserJet Pro M402dw black-and-white laser printer can be purchased online for around $249 from www.hp.com.

Mid and High-Volume Network Printers

Mid and high-volume network printers are designed for businesses that need the capacity to print a moderate to large volume of pages on a monthly basis, and they are usually best when your firm needs a printer that can produce more than 2,000 to 5,000 pages or more per month. These devices contain hardware that can handle the volume load and are built to print constantly.

The HP LaserJet Enterprise M506n printer is for those firms that need to be able to print between 2,000 and 7,500 pages per month. This printer handles moderate print volumes with ease and sends the first page out in as fast as 5.9

seconds, and prints as fast as 45 pages per minute. The printer comes with a standard input capacity of 650 sheets, one paper tray and 512 MB of memory. The embedded gigabit Ethernet network adapter allows the device to connect to the local network, and has the option to upgrade the device to support wireless connectivity with the HP Jetdirect 3000w NFC/Wireless Accessory. For the cost and performance, you cannot beat this mid-range printer, if its capabilities fit your firm's printing needs. The HP LaserJet Enterprise M506n printer can be purchased online for $649.99 from www.hp.com.

The HP LaserJet Enterprise MFP M631h multifunction printer is ideal for firms that print large volumes of documents on a monthly basis. This printer has a recommended monthly printing volume of 5,000 to 30,000 pages and prints up to 55 pages per minute. The printer comes with a standard input capacity of 800 sheets, one paper tray, 1.5 GB of memory, and an embedded gigabit Ethernet network adapter to attach the printer to your local network. The network connectivity is upgradeable to support wireless networks, a must-have option for those firms that use a wireless infrastructure for their local network. It should be noted that the printer doesn't come with a USB cable, which will have to be purchased separately if you want to connect the printer directly to a computer. This printer also supports Apple's AirPrint service, allowing users to print directly from their iPad, iPhone, or iPod Touch device if you purchase the wireless option.

For future compatibility, this printer is IPv6 (internet Protocol version 6) ready, although we have yet to see any clients running IPv6 only. For added security, this printer supports network authentication (LDAP, SMTP) that lets administrators control device access and secure print jobs through user authentication.

The printer comes with a one-year, next-business-day onsite warranty. It is compatible with both Mac and Windows-based networks, including Windows 10. A CD-ROM that contains both printer driver files and software necessary to manage and configure the device is included; in addition, the necessary software can be downloaded from HP's website. The HP LaserJet Enterprise MFP M631h multi-function printer is available online for around $2,799.99 from one of HP's resellers. At this cost, you may want to investigate using your digital copier as a printer, depending on your anticipated monthly print volume and cost per page.

Color Network Printers

Color network printers are essential for any law firm or small business that wants to print a significant volume of documents in color. If the color printer is networked, multiple users can have access to the shared resource, which is far more cost effective than giving everyone a color printer. HP is still the leading manufacturer of color printers in terms of value, selection, overall reliability, and performance. Its color LaserJet printers are reasonably priced and produce high-quality color documents.

For a small business or law firm, the HP Color LaserJet Enterprise M553x printer is perfect for everyday color printing. This printer prints up to 40 pages per minute in black and white or in color and has a recommended monthly volume of 2,000 to 6,000 pages. Its first-page-out speed of less than 7 seconds means that the color print job starts almost as soon as you issue the print command. The standard input capacity is 1,200 sheets, and the printer supports all paper sizes and is upgradeable with an envelope feeder.

The printer comes standard with 1 GB of memory and an embedded gigabit Ethernet network adapter that enables the printer to connect to your local network. If necessary, the memory is upgradeable to a maximum of 2 GB. The printer's drivers support both Mac and Windows-based systems, including Windows 10, and the printer can be networked for easy accessibility. The printer comes with a one-year onsite limited warranty.

The HP Color LaserJet M553x printer is available online for around $1,199.99 (before discounts) from HP's webstore. At the time of this writing, the printer is on sale for $999.99. Please note that the printer does not come with a USB cable, which users will have to purchase separately. That shouldn't be a problem since you will probably connect this printer to a network and not directly to a computer.

The largest operational cost for a color laser printer is the consumables. Color cartridges are not cheap, and color prints can be very expensive. One configuration point to make on all computers networked to your color printers: change the default color setting to black. This will save on the printing and subsequent waste of color cartridges for unnecessary color copies. Users can always override the setting when a color printout is required.

Digital copier manufacturers are beginning to take over the task of color printing. Investigate using a color copier for your color print needs versus a stand-alone color printer, or if you have a large-scale color print job, you may want to consider the costs of outsourcing the project to your local copier store. You might be surprised at the amount of money you could save.

Typically, lawyers lease their copiers. As you work with your copier lessor, which normally provides your supplies, make sure you negotiate a low cost per color copy and pay only for the number of pages that you print. Don't pay for the consumables (e.g., toner cartridges) or maintenance, as these should be included as part of the per-page cost.

Multifunctional Printers/Copiers

Multifunctional printers (MFPs) offer the capability to print, scan, copy, and fax from the same device, combining the functions of multiple devices into just one and eliminating the need to purchase them separately. In the long run, purchasing or leasing an MFP can save you the time and money often expended to upgrade and service multiple devices.

MFPs are very expensive and are generally leased because of the high cost to purchase. When looking at whether to buy or lease MFPs, keep some functionality questions in mind:

- Do you want the ability to print in color as well as in black and white?
- Do you need duplex printing?
- Do you want to scan documents to your hard drive, user box, or email?
- Do you want incoming faxes to be sent to email as an image file or just printed?
- Do you want to be able to link the use of the MFP to the firm's billing program?
- What printing capacity do you need?
- Do you need any finishing capabilities (e.g., stapling, folding, three-hole punch)?
- Can users print to the device using their tablet or mobile phone?
- Do you need to implement any security on the unit, and if so, what?
- At the end of your lease, can the hard drive be securely wiped or erased?

The answers to these questions will give your vendors enough detail to provide you with the MFP device that best meets the firm's needs. Your digital copier may already have some of these features installed but not configured. Check with your vendor to see what capabilities your current copier has. In our office, we have a Konica Minolta Bizhub C224e MFP device. It allows us to print both in color and in black and white at speeds up to 22 pages per minute; to scan to hard drive, user box, email, or FTP; and to fax documents, although we do not use that feature. We are able to download our scanned documents from a built-in secure internal website as JPG, PDF, XPS, or TIFF files, as well as scan to an internal email address—which we constantly use. This device has a 3,650-sheet max capacity with dual scanning speeds up to 160 pages per minute.

The Bizhub has advanced security features such as job erase, hard drive sanitizing and lock, user authentication and account tracking, Internet Protocol (IP) address filtering, and secure print and scan encryption. Plus, there are options for biometric and proximity card authentication, should we ever need these advanced security features. Needless to say, the Bizhub provides us with a secure MFP option. We are huge fans—this is our second model of one of these devices and we're looking forward to a new lease for our third unit. These devices typically can be leased for several hundred dollars ($300 to $500) per month or more.

CHAPTER FIVE

Scanners

Almost as common as printers, scanners have become a necessary piece of equipment in most offices, as more paper documents are being scanned and stored electronically. The drive to a paperless office is still very much under way. The setup and operation of scanners has become simple to the point where even the most novice computer user can do it. Many of the tasks that once had to be performed manually are now automated, and in most cases, the hookup entails connecting a single wire—or none, in the event of a wireless mobile scanner, which we discuss below.

Not often do we have to install software or drivers anymore, now that preloaded drivers are prevalent. Network scanners, however, are a little more complex to set up, and configuring them may require the assistance of your IT staff or your IT consultant.

Most desktop scanners communicate with the computer through the USB interface and come with a variety of software to assist in the scanning and file conversion process. Some models come standard with optical character recognition (OCR) software that will read the scanned image and produce a document that is both editable and searchable. Fujitsu is a manufacturer of home and business-grade scanners that have been consistently rated the best models for businesses.

Some law firms may already have scanning capability in their digital copier. As we previously stated, check with your vendor to see if scanning with your copier is a more cost-effective solution than purchasing another standalone scanner, especially for the occasional scanning job.

Mobile Scanner

The Fujitsu ScanSnap iX100 wireless scanner is the perfect, portable scanner for the mobile lawyer. This mobile device includes a lithium-ion rechargeable battery that can scan up to 260 letter-size documents on a single charge and weighs only 14 ounces. It can scan a single-side color document at 300 dots per inch in just 5.2 seconds. The ScanSnap iX100 is equipped with built-in Wi-Fi to automatically detect the wireless network. In the event you don't have a wireless network or access point, you can use Direct Connect mode to scan wirelessly between the device and your computer system.

This device comes with many different scanning options, allowing the user to "Scan to Folder," "Scan to Email," and a variety of cloud-based options such as "Scan to Dropbox," "Scan to Evernote," and "Scan to Google Drive," to name a few. You can even scan directly to your mobile device. This device is compatible with both Mac and Windows-based computers and comes with a one-year limited warranty. The ScanSnap iX100 wireless scanner can be purchased online from an Authorized Fujitsu Retailer for around $200.

Low-Volume Scanner

The Fujitsu ScanSnap iX500 Desktop Scanner is a great value for a solid automatic document feeder (ADF) scanner. This desktop scanner scans up to 25 color pages per minute, has an ADF capacity of 50 sheets, and can handle both legal and letter-sized paper. It has a maximum scanning resolution of 600 × 600 dpi and connects to the computer via the USB 3.0 interface, which is responsible for the increase in scanning speed. The scanner also comes with a built-in wireless adapter, allowing you to scan directly to a computer or mobile device without the need of a cable. It is compatible with Windows 10 and Mac OS X v10.6 or newer. This scanner comes with bundled software that includes Nuance Power PDF Standard for Windows, Nuance PDF Converter for Mac, and ABBYY FineReader. In late 2016, ScanSnap dropped the inclusion of Adobe Acrobat for Nuance's PDF software alternative.

A new feature of this scanner is the ability to scan to the cloud. With the free ScanSnap Connect app, users can link their ScanSnap to their iPad, iPhone, or Android mobile device for viewing on the go. Users also have the ability to scan to Evernote, Google Docs, Dropbox, and Google Drive, to name a few. Again, as with all cloud services, please use caution and seek the advice of your IT staff when moving client data to the cloud to ensure that your documents are secure.

The scanner comes with a standard one-year limited warranty that can be upgraded to the Advanced Exchange Service program. The Fujitsu ScanSnap iX500 Desktop Scanner can be purchased online from Fujitsu's website (www.fujitsu.com) for $495.

High-Volume Scanner

The Fujitsu fi-5530C2 is perfect for legal professionals who need a high-speed scanner on a modest budget and are serious about scanning documents. The built-in ADF holds 100 pages and scans up to 50 pages per minute (100 images) in 200 dpi in color, mono-chrome, and grayscale. This scanner comes standard with 64 MB of memory and advanced software tools to allow administrators to centrally manage the scanner more productively and cost effectively.

Using the Fujitsu fi-5530C2 scanner, a TWAIN compliant scanner, you can convert any document to Adobe PDF using either Adobe Acrobat or Nuance Power PDF software, which are not included with the purchase of this scanner. Luckily, most lawyers already have access to this software. TWAIN is an applications programming interface (API) and communications protocol that regulates communication between software and digital imaging devices, whose Working Group has been around now for almost 25 years. In summary, this means that the scanner can work with any other TWAIN compliant software for scanning documents and sending files to. Unbelievably, TWAIN actually stands for "Technology Without an Interesting Name." Add that to your did-you-know memory bank.

This scanner can handle a vigorous duty cycle of up to 4,000 documents per day and can handle documents ranging in size from a business card to a legal document without issue. The Ultra SCSI and USB 2.0 interface allows for simplified connectivity to your computer. The scanner is compatible with Microsoft Windows 10 computer systems and Windows Server 2016. It should be noted that this scanner is not compatible with Macs. The Fujitsu fi-5530C2 scanner is available online through one of Fujitsu's resellers for around $2,500 and comes with a three-month onsite limited warranty.

This amount of money is a lot for a solo or small firm operation to spend, especially on a scanner. We are sure that your digital copier could provide a less expensive solution for your scanning needs, especially if you have a newer unit that provides a convenient ability to scan to email—which this ScanSnap device does not offer. Consider that before you make a purchasing decision and you might be able to save yourself a lot of money.

CHAPTER SIX

Servers

Many small law firms struggle with the decision of whether to purchase a server. For most the struggle is with the cost of the hardware. The truth is that most firms are not solely cloud-based and are more of a hybrid type, with some applications or services hosted in the cloud and some hosted locally. Even a hybrid approach requires an on-premise ("on-prem") server where users can store their data and applications and where hosted services can be accessed. If a small firm opts against centralized storage or a single point of administration, the costs to support and maintain a decentralized computer network (peer-to-peer) will surely be much higher and is certainly not recommended. If you elect to base your practice primarily on cloud services, perhaps you only need local storage (e.g. a Network Attached Storage solution) instead of a physical server. We assume that the analysis and decision to purchase a server has already been made, hence the recommendations are listed here.

Once a server is purchased, configured, and installed, routine maintenance is all that should be required, with the hardware running like a well-oiled machine. There may be some sticker shock with the upfront cost to purchase a server, but over time, the support costs should be considerably less than if you opted not to purchase one and went with a peer-to-peer solution. The good news is that hardware costs keep coming down, so a server for a solo or small firm operation is even more affordable as time advances.

The purchase of a server is one of the most important and expensive decisions you will have to make regarding technology for your firm. A server is the mothership of the network, so the purchase decision should be made very carefully. It is absolutely not the time to be penny wise and pound foolish. The choice of a server is a business decision—make no mistake about that—and if made with great consideration and thought, it will allow your business to be more efficient from a technology perspective.

Like workstations and laptops, servers come in every make, model, and flavor. Unlike workstations, however, servers are expensive and can consume a large chunk of your technology budget rather quickly. Your firm will need to plan carefully when selecting a server—including discussing future needs and goals—so that the desirable hardware and software components can be identified. Be careful when planning, because you don't want to have to buy a new server every other year. The average life span of a server is at least four to five years (it is difficult to get warranty coverage beyond five years)—so start planning (and budgeting) well in advance!

Solo—File and Printer-Sharing

The most simple and basic reason for getting a server is for file and printer sharing. Centralizing electronic file storage and administration and installation of printers will save you time, money, and headaches when it comes to maintaining and managing your network. Some servers are designed specifically for the purpose of sharing files, documents, and printers. These servers come with basic hardware and software and are relatively inexpensive when compared to the mid-range to higher-end servers.

The Dell PowerEdge T330 server provides small businesses with the most basic file and print-sharing capabilities. The following table provides the server's hardware and software components, along with some technical specifications.

File- and Printer-Sharing Server

Hardware Component	Recommendation
Model:	Dell PowerEdge T330
Chassis:	Tower
Operating System:	Windows Server 2016 Standard Edition
Processors:	Intel Xeon E3-1270 v5, 3.6 GHz, 8 MB Cache
Memory:	32 GB UDIMM, 2400 MT/s DDR4
RAID Controller:	PERC S130
Hard Drive Configuration:	RAID 5
Hard Drives:	Three 480 GB Solid State Drive
Network Adapter:	Onboard Broadcom 5720 Dual Port 1 GB LOM
Warranty:	Five-year ProSupport and next-business-day on-site service
Other:	DVD+/−RW Drive

This Dell PowerEdge T330 was customized through Dell's website (www.dell.com) and contains an Intel Xeon 3.6 GHz processor with 32 GB of RAM. This server comes with the Windows Server 2016 Standard Edition operating system. CALs (client access licenses) are needed for each device or user that accesses the server. The three 480 GB Solid State Drives are configured in a RAID 5 (redundant array of independent disks) hard drive configuration for increased performance and fault tolerance. In a RAID 5 hard drive configuration, if one of the hard drives were to fail, the server would continue to operate until the failed hard drive could be replaced. In most other hard drive configurations, if a server's hard drive were to fail, the server would be inoperable until the disk was repaired or replaced. The RAID 5 configuration offers both fault tolerance with the parity hard drive and better performance than most other RAID or mirrored disk configurations. RAID 5 hard drive configurations are strongly recommended for all law firm servers.

In total, this server has about one terabyte of hard drive space available for the storage of electronic data, programs, and other applications. The onboard dual gigabit network adapters will allow clients to connect to the server at gigabit speeds, assuming the rest of your network components (switches, cabling) are gigabit as well.

One of the most important features to consider when purchasing a server is the warranty. In most cases, you will not need both the hardware and software support. At a minimum, you must include a hardware warranty that will cover the hardware and labor cost to replace any of the components that may fail during the server's life span. This Dell PowerEdge server comes with a five-year, next-business-day on-site parts and labor warranty at an included cost of about $575 when bundled with the server hardware. Having a hardware warranty for your server is critical to protecting your equipment, data, and business. This is no time to be miserly. This Dell PowerEdge T330 server was available on Dell's website for approximately $2,575 at the time of this writing.

Small Firm—File and Printer-Sharing/ Hosting Services

When purchasing a server for your network, you must decide what function the server will have in your day-to-day business operations. In addition to file and printer sharing, it is common for small firms to host their company's email. Although you can also host a website, we recommend that you outsource that to a website hosting provider because of potential security, administration, and resource issues. The added hosting services (email and/or web) will require a server with upgraded hardware to be able to provide the necessary resources for the services to operate reliably.

The Dell PowerEdge T630 provides small firms and businesses a cost-effective solution to hosting their own email or website. The following table provides the server's hardware and software components, along with some technical specifications.

File and Printer-Sharing/Hosting Services

Hardware Component	Recommendation
Model:	Dell PowerEdge T630
Chassis:	Tower
Operating System:	Windows Server 2016 Standard Edition
Processors:	Dual Intel Xeon E5-2640 v4 2.4 GHz, 25 M Cache
Memory:	64 GB RDIMM, 2400 MT/s, Dual Rank
Primary Controller Card:	S130
Hard Drive Configuration:	RAID 5
Hard Drives:	Three 2 TB 7.2K RPM SATA 6 Gbps 3.5-Inch
Network Adapter:	Onboard Intel i350-AM2 Dual Port 1 GB LOM
Warranty:	Five-year ProSupport and Next Business Day On-Site Service
Other:	Redundant power supply, DVD+/−RW drive

This Dell PowerEdge T630 was customized through Dell's website. It contains Dual Intel Xeon 2.4 GHz processors with 64 GB of memory. The server was customized in a tower chassis; however, the same model is available in a rack-mount chassis for an additional $65. The rack-mount chassis is for those firms and small businesses that maintain their servers and networking equipment in a rack. The processors will supply more than enough horsepower to configure the server as an email or web server, and the 64 GB of memory will allow these services to run smoothly and will prevent the server from lagging or becoming bogged down.

The server comes with Windows Server 2016 Standard Edition pre-installed. CALs will need to be purchased for each device and/or user that wishes to connect to the server. Dell offers device or user CALs bundled with the server purchase for a price of $24.58 per CAL.

The three 2 TB SATA hard drives are configured in a RAID 5 hard drive configuration and provide about 4 TB of storage space for your firm's applications and data. This PowerEdge server comes with the five-year Pro-Support and next business day on-site hardware warranty. The Dell PowerEdge T630 server was available on Dell's website for approximately $6,275 at the time of this writing.

Don't forget to consider backup software and any additional applications (e.g., security software, file synchronization, encryption) when configuring the server, because you might get a better discount from the vendor if they are bundled and purchased with the server hardware.

Small Firm—Database/Applications Server

Your firm's software requirements, current and future, will play a big role in determining what hardware and software components your server will need to adequately support your firm in the coming years. So far, we have discussed the hardware and software specifications for a server used primarily for file and printer sharing and one capable of handling basic hosting services, such as email and a website. When planning to use a server to host a database application, case management software, or e-discovery software, you must look at the minimum requirements for each piece of software and then go above and beyond the specifications that vendors provide. The bare minimum requirements listed by vendors need to be regarded cautiously. To run well and reliably, the software almost always requires more horsepower.

The recommended Dell PowerEdge T630 server is capable of handling most database and software applications as long as it contains advanced hardware to handle the powerful and robust database applications. The server's hardware and software components are provided in the following table.

Database/Applications Server

Hardware Component	Recommendation
Model:	Dell PowerEdge T630
Chassis:	Tower
Operating System:	Windows Server 2016 Standard Edition

Processors:	Dual Intel Xeon E5-2695 v4 2.1 GHz, 45 M Cache, 9.6GT/s QPI, Turbo
Memory:	128 GB RDIMM, 2400 MT/s, Dual Rank
Primary Controller Card:	PERC H730 RAID Controller
Hard Drive Configuration:	RAID 5
Hard Drives:	Three 2 TB 7.2K RPM SATA 3.5-Inch
Network Adapter:	Onboard Intel i350-AM2 Dual Port 1 GB LOM
Warranty:	Five-year ProSupport and Mission Critical 4Hr 7/24 on-site service
Other:	Dual, hot-plug, redundant power supply 1100W, DVD+/−RW Drive

The PowerEdge T630 server was customized through Dell's website and contains Dual Intel Xeon E5-2695 v4 2.1 GHz processors and 128 GB of memory. The processor is faster than the processor included with the server discussed in the previous section, with a much larger cache. This server comes with the Windows Server 2016 Standard Edition operating system.

The three 2 TB hard drives are configured in a RAID 5 hard disk configuration and provide about 4 TB of storage space for applications and data. If the system needs more storage space or faster disk read/write speeds, these configurations can be set, especially if you plan to use virtualization (explained in the following section).

The redundant power supply allows the server to stay powered on in the event that one of the power supplies fails. The server comes with dual embedded Broadcom Ethernet adapters, providing connectivity for up to two networks. The PowerEdge server comes with a five-year ProSupport Mission Critical 4HR 7 × 24 on-site hardware warranty, which provides three years of four-hour response, same-day parts and labor warranty. The Dell PowerEdge T630 server was available on Dell's website for approximately $12,500 at the time of this writing. You can save a little money if you want the next-day warranty instead of the four-hour response warranty.

Virtual Servers

The large push within the IT industry continues to be toward virtualization bundled with cloud services. Microsoft continues to sell more licenses for virtual machines than it does for physical hardware. This is one trend that isn't going to reverse.

Simply put, virtualization means that a single piece of hardware contains and hosts multiple server or desktop images, otherwise known as machines. Virtualization enables the consolidation of data and applications onto a single physical hardware server. The reduction in hardware saves energy, management, and administration effort and reduces overall hardware and software costs, along with rack space, especially if your firm needs multiple servers.

Virtualization is used to separate hosting services and applications, creating independent machines, which allows for one virtual server to be down for maintenance without affecting the others. For example, if Windows updates were downloaded onto a virtual server hosting file and print-sharing services, this virtual server could be rebooted and have the updates applied without having to bring down or affect the entire host system, keeping other virtual servers online and available to users. It also means that you can quickly "spool up" a virtual machine for testing new applications or services without investing in additional hardware. Virtual servers are also very flexible and can be modified on the fly. Resources (e.g., RAM, disk space, processing power) can be modified while the virtual machine is running. Running short on disk space? No problem. Just go to the management console and add a few hundred gigabytes to the virtual machine's dynamic disk.

Previously, virtualization was not implemented due to the required costs, expertise, and large budget. It was not typically found in a small firm environment; however, this is no longer true. We are recommending that small firms consider virtualization technologies when making server hardware and software purchasing decisions, especially in scenarios where the firm is hosting services such as email internally.

Is server virtualization the best choice for your network environment? Probably, but see the advice which follows.

What services and applications are running on your network? If your network is running Microsoft Exchange Server, SQL Server, and a case management application, most likely you will need multiple servers to host all of these services and software. Most case management applications now require a separate server to run on. By using virtualization, you can avoid purchase of another physical hardware server by installing the case management software on its own virtual server, as long as your virtual server meets, if not exceeds, the host specifications required by the vendor of the software.

When purchasing a host system (the server hosting the virtual servers), the most critical hardware options to consider are the amount of memory, number and type of processors, and amount of storage space. For each virtual server, 8 GB or more of memory must be allocated for the virtual server to operate. A larger amount of memory will be needed if the virtual server is hosting a database or other memory-hungry service.

This does not account for the amount of memory that the host system will require. For example, if you have a host server running three virtual servers, you will need a minimum of 32 GB or more of memory installed in the host server to supply the host and all of the virtual servers with enough memory resources to operate. To accommodate the necessary hardware, the host system must be running at least the Windows Server 2016 Standard Edition operating system.

When running virtual servers, you will need to ensure that the host system has enough processing capability to handle the processing load. At a minimum, you will want the system to contain Intel Xeon processors with a processing speed of 2.1 GHz or faster. The optimum solution for stand-alone servers is to use Intel Xeon processors with the same speed range, and in virtualization solutions, you will need to have multiple processors with multiple cores.

The Xeon processors that are in the servers recommended previously were designed by Intel for virtualization solutions, providing increased virtualization security, reduced storage and network latencies, and acceleration of fundamental virtualization processes throughout the system. The multicore processors combine two or more cores onto a single integrated circuit, providing multiprocessing capabilities to the chip. Multiprocessing allows the execution of multiple concurrent software processes in a system, which is vital in a virtualization solution.

The amount of storage space required to run all of the virtual servers and the host system will vary from solution to solution. When determining the amount of storage space the systems will require, you need to consider the services and applications that are in use. For example, a virtual server hosting Microsoft Exchange Server will require enough disk space to account for the current size and future growth of the Exchange Database stores along with the program files and operating system. If more space is needed at a later time, the amount of storage space allocated to each virtual server can be independently configured and modified in real time.

For ease of configuration and setup, bearing the cost of additional hard drive storage up front makes more sense than waiting to add more hard drives later. Plus, it's always recommended that the host system and virtual servers have available more than enough hard drive space, so problems with low disk space can be avoided. We have clients who have terabytes of disk space available just for their file and printer-sharing virtual server, given how cheap it is to increase the storage capacity. As an alternative to purchasing host-based storage, you may want to look into a storage area network (SAN) device that would provide locally attached storage over a dedicated network, usually over Fibre Channel or iSCSI.

Microsoft offers free server virtualization solutions for Windows Server 2016. For host systems running Windows Server 2016, Microsoft has included the Hyper-V virtualization system with the base installation of the operating system, and this role is installed through the Server Roles interface. Hyper-V enables the consolidation of multiple server roles as separate virtual servers running on a single host system, allowing for different operating systems such as Linux, Windows, and others to run in parallel. For more information regarding Microsoft's virtualization solutions, you can visit Microsoft's website at https://www.microsoft.com/en-us/cloud-platform/virtualization.

Hyper-V was designed with enhanced security features in mind, providing an architecture that is less vulnerable to attack. This software includes a set of management and administration tools that can manage the host and virtual systems' hardware from the same interface. It even allows administrators to migrate live systems from server to server. Windows Server 2016 has an updated version of Microsoft's Hyper-V, which includes such new features as discrete device assignment, encryption support for the operating system disk and host resource protection. You can read more about the new features of Hyper-V Server 2016 at https://docs.microsoft.com/en-us/windows-server/virtualization/hyper-v/what-s-new-in-hyper-v-on-windows.

Depending on the operating system of the host system, a few Microsoft-based software options are available for server virtualization, and they are fully supported. We have observed that the Hyper-V implementations may have some issues sharing peripheral devices across the virtual machines. As an example, you may not be able to share the USB ports of the hardware with a virtual machine without some kind of workaround, which means that you can't copy files from a USB flash drive from the host system to the virtual system. There are third-party applications that use USB over IP which provides a workaround for this issue.

Software licensing will also play a role in determining your firm's ability to move to a virtualization environment. To say the licensing is easy to figure out when it comes to virtualization would be a flat-out lie. Microsoft has muddied the waters when it comes to virtualization licensing, because it varies depending on the type of server operating system and the number of processors. Some operating system editions allow you to use the license key on the host and on up to two virtual machines. If you're running a host with Windows Server 2016 Datacenter Edition, you get a feature called Automated Virtual Machine Activation. With this feature, any virtual machine on this host running Windows Server 2016 will automatically activate.

There are other alternatives to Microsoft's virtualization solutions, such as VMware's vSphere Hypervisor (ESXi). If you are investigating alternative virtualization solutions, you will need to work with your IT vendor to see what other options might be available. We currently recommend and use the VMware solution instead of Microsoft's Hyper-V solution. VMware has been in the virtualization game a lot longer than Microsoft, and it is a lot easier to share those USB ports with the virtual machines. VMware Tools also offers some other useful and time-saving administration capabilities.

What we do know is this: The cost to purchase the hardware and software necessary to implement a virtualization environment for your network will be significantly less than the cost of purchasing multiple physical servers to fill the necessary roles your applications and services require.

Peer-to-Peer Network

Many small firms use the built-in peer-to-peer network capabilities of their computer systems as an alternative to purchasing a server. A peer-to-peer network, in its simplest form, is two or more computers that are able to communicate with one another to share files and folders, printers, and applications without using a server to accomplish these tasks. Peer-to-peer networks are commonly used in solo or small firm offices with only two or three computers. The computers, located on the same local network and belonging to the same Workgroup (Microsoft's name for a peer-to-peer network), can access shared resources in the Workgroups to which they are joined. Unless a computer is joined to a domain (typically used on large networks for central administration), it belongs to a Workgroup. The default Workgroup name in Windows 7, 8, and 10 is the original WORKGROUP, but you are free to name your workgroup something that may be more appropriate.

Peer-to-peer networks may sound like a good solution for small firms that have only a few computers, but this type of network has some significant disadvantages compared to purchasing a server. First, when networking computers together, you are going to experience a slowdown and inconsistency in your system's performance. Workstations are not designed to handle concurrent access to their files by other computers. When this occurs, the system's resources are severely taxed, causing disruption to the users. Think of this as a tug-of-war for data. Your computer is trying to use data at the same time that someone else needs it. Because of the inconsistency and unreliability of the peer-to-peer network, corruption of shared files, such as case management and billing systems, occurs frequently. Since computers in a peer-to-peer network can be running different operating systems, software incompatibilities between the systems can occur. Management of user accounts, along with implementing the proper security controls to protect sensitive and confidential data, becomes a nightmare—and even more difficult should a breach occur that requires investigation.

The decentralization of critical firm data can lead to unnecessarily complex data backup scenarios, often resulting in important data not being backed up or protected. On top of all the issues above, the need to manage and administer multiple copies of the same software, such as antivirus protection on each individual computer, becomes needlessly tiresome and time-consuming. Software that is centrally managed is much more cost effective to purchase and maintain, as opposed to managing each computer's software suites independently. Just figure in the added administration costs that your firm will pay its IT provider; this will more than cover the cost of a server—and then some!

There is an inaccurate perception that peer-to-peer networks save money and cost less than client/server networks. However, in the end, this is never the case. Yes, purchasing a server—even a lower-end unit—might seem expensive at first, but the costs of managing and maintaining a peer-to-peer network will always be higher than the costs you would have incurred if you had implemented a server/client network in the first place.

The software licensing costs for peer-to-peer networks can be higher because you are purchasing single licenses. Software that is administered and maintained on independent computers will take more time than if it were centrally managed from a server. Technical support and consulting costs will be much higher in a peer-to-peer environment, a fact that is usually not considered when making the initial decision to purchase and use a peer-to-peer network. For most small network environments, even those involving as few as two computers, purchasing a server to centralize applications and data can save time and money—and the number of headaches you will have to endure in the long run.

CHAPTER SEVEN

Server Operating Systems

Choosing the hardware components is just one step in selecting the right server for your business. The next step is determining what operating system and software will best meet the current and future needs of the firm. There are many variations of server operating systems currently available for both Windows and Mac servers, and they are described in detail in the following sections.

Microsoft Windows Server 2012 R2

Windows Server 2012 R2, released in October 2013, was the successor to Windows Server 2012. Like its predecessor, Windows Server 2012 R2 was released in four editions: Foundation, Essentials, Standard, and Datacenter.

Some of the changes from Windows Server 2012 that were introduced in Windows Server 2012 R2 included:

- Automated tiering of frequently accessed files on the fastest physical media
- De-duplication for Virtual Hard Drives
- New version of Windows PowerShell (v4)
- Integrated Office 365 support
- Return of the Windows Start Button
- UEFI-based virtual machines
- Boot from SCSI device option
- Faster VM deployment (50 percent increase in speed reported)

Microsoft Windows Server 2016

Microsoft Windows Server 2016 is the latest server operating system from Microsoft and is the successor to Windows Server 2012. Microsoft developed this operating system concurrently with Windows 10. This edition was released on September 26, 2016, at Microsoft's Ignite conference and became generally available in October of 2016.

Some of the new features of the latest operating system include:

- A new version of Windows PowerShell (v5.1)
- Internet Information Services 10
- Integration of Windows Defender
- Improved remote desktop services, including performance and stability improvements
- Active Directory Federation Services
- Soft Restart—a feature to speed up the booting process

Microsoft has included a new installation option called Nano Server, which offers a minimal installation footprint and excludes a graphical interface, support for 32-bit software, and console login. All management of this server is performed through the Windows Management Instrumentation interface and PowerShell. Early testing showed that the Nano Server resulted in 90 percent fewer critical security advisories and required 80 percent less reboots than a standard installation of Windows Server.

This operating system has been around for a few years now and is a replacement for Windows Server 2012. This latest version of the operating system should be selected when purchasing/configuring a new server.

Mac OS X Server 10.10 (Yosemite)

Mac OS X Server 10.10, nicknamed Yosemite, was released in October 2014 as a downloadable package from the Mac App Store, just as the previous versions of the server software have been.

Some of the new features include an easier-than-ever ability to share data and folders between Mac, iPad, and PCs using the new superfast protocol for sharing files in OS X Server, SMB3. This new protocol helps protect against data tampering and eavesdropping by encrypting and signing data while in transmission, adding another layer of security protection to your server.

The new Profile Manager simplifies deploying, configuring, and managing Mac computers and iOS devices, including user accounts, and allows administrators the ability to perform push installs of OS X enterprise apps and iOS media assets including PDF, ePub, and iBooks Author files.

The Caching Server automatically speeds up the downloads and delivery of software updates through the App Store, Mac App Store, iTunes Store, iTunes U, and iBooks Store to users on the network whose apps need updating.

Mac OS Server 5

This version of the Mac server, first released in the fall of 2015, is the successor to the Mac OS X Server 10.10 operating system and is currently on version 5.6, released in April 2018. It should be noted that the MacOS Server 5.6 app only operates on the MacOS High Sierra (10.13.5) operating system and later. This latest version of the Mac server is accessible directly from the Mac App Store for only $19.99.

The latest version of Server 5 includes new features such as:

- Supports MacOS High Sierra 10.13 and later
- New Caching Server, Time Machine Server and File sharing advanced options are now built directly into the operating system
- Support for APFS volumes
- The Profile Manager now has support for new restrictions, payloads and management commands
- Removes File Transfer Protocol (FTP) service and support
- The ability to push out software updates to iOS 11 devices even while passcode locked
- Additional management options for MacOS High Sierra devices and users

Future releases of macOS Server will start to remove key features such as the Calendar, Contacts, DHCP, DNS, Mail, Messages and other services. Apple has released a document titled "macOS Server Service Migration Guide" (https://developer.apple.com/support/macos-server/macOS-Server-Service-Migration-Guide.pdf) to help users plan for the discontinuation of services Apple will no longer support. Specifically, this document provides a migration path for the services that Apple will be dropping support for starting in the fall of 2018. It now appears that the future of macOS can now be called into question.

If your firm is running macOS server it is time to read the tea leaves, and prepare to migrate away from this solution.

CHAPTER EIGHT

Networking Hardware

Networking hardware typically refers to equipment that allows network devices to communicate with one another, but not always. Other types of networking hardware include server racks, cabling, and other devices that help make up the computer network. Here we provide descriptions and recommendations for the most common types of networking hardware that you will require in a solo or small firm computer network.

Switches

A switch is a piece of networking hardware that connects network segments (discrete sections of the network), allowing multiple devices to communicate with one another. For example, if two or more computers are connected into the same switch and are located within the same defined network, the switch will allow these devices to communicate. Switches inspect data packets, and based on the source and destination hardware addresses, forward the data packet appropriately. Switches only transfer the packet of information to its intended recipient, saving network bandwidth, as well as preserving confidentiality, delivering the information much more quickly. In comparison, network hubs send the traffic to all ports, irrespective of the destination device, and are rarely seen in a production environment anymore. In fact, eBay may be the only place that you can purchase a hub these days. Unlike network hubs, switches are "intelligent" devices that can operate on more than one layer of the Open Systems Interconnection (OSI) model, such as a multilayer switch. Switches allow traffic to pass through them at speeds of 10 Mbps, 100 Mbps, 1 Gbps, or 10 Gbps, depending on the speeds of the ports.

The International Organization for Standardization created the OSI model as a way of subdividing a communications system into seven layers: Physical, Data Link, Network, Transport, Session, Presentation, and Application. We could write a whole book on the OSI model, but others already have.

Most solo and small law firms will not need expensive high-end network switches for their computer infrastructure. In the majority of situations, a switch is needed only to connect computer workstations to the server and to the router for internet access. Netgear offers reasonably priced switches in a variety of configurations to meet almost any solo or small firm need. Its Gigabit Unmanaged Switch series is a good choice for the solo or small law firm because of the low cost, ease of setup, and reliability. Setup of these devices requires no configuration—just plug in the power, network cables and you are ready to go.

When purchasing a switch for your firm, you will need to determine the number of connections or ports the switch will need. Next, you will have to determine the speeds of the ports that you will require. Will all of your computers need the ability to connect to the server at gigabit speeds, or will just a handful of devices need that kind of speed? Remember, you certainly will pay more for a 48-port switch with 48 gigabit ports than if you buy a 48-port switch with only two gigabit ports and 46 10/100MB ports. Given the bandwidth of today's networks and applications, it's almost a requirement to purchase a switch with gigabit ports, and the added speed is worth the additional cost. The Gigabit Unmanaged Switches from Netgear can be found on its website at www.netgear.com starting at around $100.

These switches are also offered in a 1U (single unit) rack-mount solution that will fit standard 19-inch racks and are backed by a Netgear ProSafe lifetime hardware warranty.

For those law firms that require or desire tighter security controls over their computer systems and users, a managed switch may be the solution. A managed switch, unlike an unmanaged switch, is a device that can be administered or controlled. Advanced features include the ability to limit how computer systems can "talk" with one another at the physical level (private virtual LANs), advanced performance monitoring, Layer 3–based prioritization, and increased bandwidth control. These switches also support Quality of Service (QoS), which can be used to prioritize certain network traffic over other functions, such as VoIP (voice over internet protocol) phones.

A good cost-effective managed switch for small to medium-sized law firms is the Gigabit Smart Managed Plus Switch from Netgear. This managed switch can be found on Netgear's website (www.netgear.com) starting at around $200 and can be purchased with differing numbers of ports and connection speeds, depending on the requirements. As an alternative, Dell manufactures some very cost-effective switches for network connectivity. It has managed and unmanaged versions as well as multi-gigabit port models.

Router/Firewall with IDS/IPS Capabilities

A router is a computer networking device that connects two or more independent networks—for example, your firm's local computer network and your internet service provider's (ISP) network. A router's job is to determine the proper path for data to travel between the networks and to forward data packets to the next device along the path—basically to get your data from point A to point B. Routers come in all shapes and sizes and can have different features. For a solo or small firm, the most basic router will often be sufficient to connect the local network to the Internet, as well as to protect computers and other hardware devices on the local network from outside attacks (though there is no silver-bullet solution). A basic router will require some configuration from the default values to communicate with the ISP's network, as well as to strengthen the security and protection it provides to your information systems. Most basic routers are capable of handling only broadband internet connections, such as cable and DSL, by using the Ethernet port coming from the cable or DSL modem. If your firm has a T1 (rarely seen these days) or any variant of this internet connection, your ISP will probably provide you with a router.

The increasing number of data breaches has prompted a lot of discussion recently about which router a solo or small firm should use. Whichever router your firm chooses, it must have a built-in firewall, logging capabilities, and an intrusion detection system/intrusion prevention system (IDS/IPS) module. There can be no exceptions.

An intrusion detection system (IDS) is used to detect many types of malicious network traffic and computer usage that can't be detected by a conventional firewall or router. These malicious activities include network attacks against vulnerable services (web hosting, email, databases, etc.), data-driven attacks on applications, host-based attacks such as privilege escalation, unauthorized logins, and access to sensitive files. Privilege escalation is the act of exploiting a known vulnerability in an application to gain access to re-sources that would have otherwise been protected. When an IDS and an IPS are used in combination, they also can detect and prevent malware such as viruses, Trojan horses, and worms from entering the network.

An IDS/IPS device is commonly placed at the gateway of the computer network so that all incoming and outgoing network traffic passes through it. This allows the device to scan all incoming/outgoing traffic before it is passed on to the destination located on the local computer network, denying the entry of any malicious traffic and prohibiting the exit of any malicious traffic. A firewall has the ability to permit or deny data traffic based on port number, originating or receiving internet protocol (IP) address, and protocol type, to name just a few, and it is usually based on rules that are set up and configured by an administrator. An IP address is a unique address or identifier assigned to a networked device, such as a computer, that allows the device to communicate with other networked devices. Just think of an IP address as being the same as a home address, which is a unique way to identify your home's physical location.

Today, the hackers have gotten so good at breaking into law firms that it is becoming increasingly hard to keep them out. When they do get in, they often go unnoticed for months. And be advised, nothing we recommend, however good it is, is a guarantee that your confidential data will not be breached. For this reason, there is no longer an entry-level routing solution that we can recommend with confidence. Your firm's data is just too valuable. The security mantra no longer focuses on defending the network but is now "Detect and Respond."

Given the types of data that your firm stores, such as Social Security numbers, credit card numbers, patient/medical records, and other sensitive client information, the only way to combat hackers and have a chance of keeping them out is through the implementation of a defense-in-depth security strategy. This type of information protection strategy provides security at all levels of your computer network, including the point at which your local network interfaces with the public internet. For this reason, we recommend the Cisco Meraki line of security appliances, even for a solo lawyer.

The Cisco Meraki line of security appliances provide high-performance connectivity for small businesses and have built-in threat defense, including a proven stateful (which inspects the state of the transmission) packet inspection firewall, an IDS/IPS (with Advanced Security License), and an optional content-filtering subscription package to restrict a user's access to undesirable websites that may contain malware and phishing attacks. The Cisco Meraki MX64W security appliance offers a wireless option for those firms that require it. The Cisco Meraki security appliances start at around $400 for the hardware and the Advanced Security License costs about $300 per year.

It's becoming harder to find a router for a small to medium-sized business that doesn't include wireless 802.11 capabilities, although the Cisco Meraki line has plenty of wired-only devices to choose from. Be careful when purchasing these devices for your firm's computer network, as you may unintentionally open up your network to unwanted guests if your system is not configured properly. The majority of these devices still come preconfigured with open, unsecured wireless networks—which may be acceptable for your guest network, but even most wireless devices now have an option to set up a separate guest network to keep your visitor's computer network separate from the firm's. You can never be too safe. Remember, you also have the ability to disable the wireless capability if you don't need it.

Make sure you consult with your IT vendor on best practices when implementing a wireless network for your law firm. And for heaven's sake, make sure all the default settings are changed. Even "script kiddies" know all the default settings.

Racks

A rack unit or enclosure is a piece of hardware that is used to store, organize, and secure your networking and computing equipment. Most often, rack units are used to hold rack-mount servers and network communication equipment such as firewalls and switches. Many types of computer and networking hardware are offered in rack-mount sizes, due to the need to place and secure equipment within a single physical location. Rack units can be portable units mounted on caster wheels; bolted to the floor; or, if small enough, mounted on the wall. The amount of space that is available for the servers and networking equipment will greatly affect which type of rack to purchase. The leading manufacturers of rack units and enclosures are American Power Conversion (APC) and Chatsworth.

APC NetShelter SX enclosures are rack enclosures with advanced cooling, power distribution, and cable management for server and networking devices. The 19-inch rack is vendor-neutral and is guaranteed to be compatible with all EIA-310–compliant 19-inch equipment, which covers nearly all rack-mountable equipment. The 19 inches refers to the horizontal distance between the mounting screws for the equipment. These enclosures offer large cable access slots in the roof to provide overhead cable egress, which is useful when cable runs come down through the ceiling. The bottom design allows for unobstructed cable access through a raised panel floor, which is common in network data centers. The enclosures are well ventilated with perforated front and rear doors to provide ample ventilation for servers and other networking hardware that require unobstructed airflow to keep systems cool. The front and rear doors can be arranged to open in either direction, depending on the layout of the room. For physical security protection, both of these doors can be locked.

The enclosure contains rear cable-management channels to assist in managing the plethora of cables that servers and network equipment require.

The frame design of the NetShelter SX enclosures is made with heavy-gauge mounting rails and casters to provide support for up to 3,000 pounds of equipment. APC's NetShelter SX enclosures are offered in many different sizes (stand-alone, data center, colocation, etc.) and can be purchased with accessories, such as UPS battery backups, retractable keyboard, mouse pad, flip-down monitor, cable-management arms, additional fans, and power distribution centers. The APC NetShelter SX rack enclosures can be purchased online at APC's website (www.apc.com), and the basic enclosures start at around $1,500.

If you're hesitant to spend $1,500 on a piece of equipment just to hold your servers and networking devices, you may be able to find used racks from local businesses that are moving or have been closed, or through your local online classifieds, at only a fraction of the price.

Cabling

Now that you have all of your computer equipment selected and purchased, you will need to decide how to wire your data and voice network and what type of network patch cables to purchase to connect your computers to the network drops (cables from the wall outlet to the hub/switch location). These patch cables come in various lengths and are primarily offered in two different types.

First, you have the category 5e cable, which is not the same as the generically termed Cat 5 specification. Second, you have the category 6 cable, more commonly referred to as Cat 6, along with category 7 cables used for networks requiring data transfer speeds of up to 10 Gbps. Each type of cable has a different maximum throughput speed. As with computers, newer cable standards continue to be developed that can handle greater data transfer speeds. There is even a category 8 cable that was approved in June 2016, promising a new copper speedway for data centers in the not-too-distant future, and operating up to speeds of 40 Gbps. This new specification is directed toward cabling that will be used by data centers to transport data up to four times faster than they currently do now, using the same type of cable.

The Cat 6 standard cable is now the de facto standard used by businesses, increasing in popularity as more and more networking and computer devices operate and communicate at gigabit speeds. Current data transfer rates and applications operating at speeds of 1 Gbps are starting to push the limits of category 5 cabling; although category 5e cable is rated for gigabit speeds, it should be used with caution. The trends of the past and predictions for the future indicate that data rates have been doubling every 18 months. The category 6 cables offer double the amount of bandwidth capacity of category 5 cables and a better transmission performance. The category 6 cable provides a higher signal-to-noise ratio, allowing for higher reliability for current applications and higher data rates for the future. Analysts have indicated that the majority of new wiring installations are using Cat 6 cabling. This decision is fairly easy because all Cat 6 cabling is backward compatible with Cat 5e cabling.

Just when we thought that we would be limited to 1 Gbps speeds with the current cabling in our office, the IEEE (Institute of Electrical and Electronic Engineers) has approved the 802.3bz standard. The standard was specifically designed to bridge the gap between 1 Gbps (Cat 5e and Cat 6) and 10 Gbps (Cat 6a or 7) and provides for 2.5 Gbps over Cat 5e cable and 5 Gbps over Cat 6 cable. We are slowly starting to see a whole new line of networking products (e.g., switches, routers, etc.) supporting 2.5 Gbps and 5 Gbps connections. We will soon see if these new devices start to take off!

Category 7 cabling is only commonly seen in data centers and is not yet widely used in local networks. If your firm is planning on wiring the office for data and voice, it makes all the sense in the world to wire with Cat 6 cabling. Remember, once the dust has settled from the construction, it would be extremely costly to have any type of cabling pulled out and replaced. The approximately 10 percent premium that you currently will pay for Cat 6 cabling over Cat 5e cabling is worth the added cost. As time goes on, the premium is getting smaller and smaller.

Wireless Networking Devices

A wireless networking device allows for communication between devices that are not physically connected by wires or network cables. In a solo or small firm, if the cost to wire an office space with data cables is too expensive, a wireless solution may be the answer. Plus, who wants networking cables all over the place? This is particularly true in older properties—and may be aesthetically desirable in historic buildings. A wireless network is extremely convenient for lawyers who use laptops, smartphones, or tablets because they can move from their office to the conference room with these devices and still stay connected to the local network and internet. However, we do not recommend wireless connections while connecting to a database or database applications such as some case management systems. Wireless connections could cause database corruption, which would require a reload of backup data. The cost to purchase a wireless networking device is extremely low, and the benefits gained are worth the small investment. However, do not implement a wireless network without taking the proper security precautions. By default, most wireless routers and access points are preconfigured without encryption being enabled. This means that by default, all communications between computers and the wireless networking device are unencrypted and therefore insecure. How many people have connected their laptop to an unencrypted wireless network so that they could check their email or perform online banking? We see this all the time—even at legal technology conferences!

Wireless networks should be set up with the proper security. First and foremost, encryption should be enabled on the wireless device. You should have separate wireless networks for guests—and the guest network needs to be secured with encryption! A major change to wireless encryption is the approval of the WPA3 standard. Expect to see devices supporting this new standard arriving throughout 2019.

Most wireless devices ship to end users with an unencrypted network or a network encrypted using the wired equivalent privacy (WEP) 64-bit or 128-bit algorithm. Ultimately, neither of these solutions is adequate. WEP is a weak encryption algorithm that can be cracked in a matter of minutes using free open-source software. Do not use WEP! Frankly, the Federal Trade Commission and the Canadian Privacy Commissioner have both found WEP encryption insufficient to secure credit card information. Some time ago, Wi-Fi protected access (WPA) using the TKIP (temporal key integrity protocol) algorithm was cracked by a group of Japanese scientists in about a minute. So avoid WPA as well. This means that you should be encrypting using WPA2 only. However, WPA2 has recently been the subject of a severe vulnerability known as KRACK (Key Reinstallation Attacks), which means your Wi-Fi device is probably impacted. Vendors have rapidly reacted to this latest report by providing fixes for the attack. Make sure your wireless devices has the update applied to address the KRACK attacks.

WPA3 is a new wireless standard that will soon replace WPA2, offering more secure encryption features and processes than its predecessor. First and most importantly, WPA3 implements individualized data encryption when you connect to open Wi-Fi networks, protecting the traffic between your wireless device and the access point from "snooping" without first cracking the encryption. This is a huge, huge upgrade to the security of public Wi-Fi hot spots (this should have been fixed MANY years ago!). WPA3 includes a feature to simplify the process of configuring security for devices that have limited or no display interface. How the industry will implement this is unknown, but it offers hope for more seamless and secure wireless connections to Wi-Fi networks. This is great news for those users that travel often!

If the wireless network is for the firm only, enable MAC (media access control) filtering on the wireless device. MAC filtering essentially limits the devices that may communicate with the wireless device. If the MAC address of a computer's wireless network card does not match an authorized MAC address, then the wireless device will not be allowed to connect. Enabling MAC filtration will also stop employees from connecting their personal smartphones to the wireless network without authorization, even if they know the appropriate network name and passphrase. This is an added layer of security. Most commonly, wireless routers and access points ship with default network names such as Linksys or Netgear. While in operation, these devices will broadcast their names so that wireless clients can locate the wireless networks. It is strongly recommended, for security reasons, that the default name of the wireless network be changed (not to something identifying who you are—such as TheSmithLawFirm) and that SSID (service set identifier, which is essentially the network name) broadcasting be disabled.

If your router doesn't come equipped with built-in wireless support, there are other wireless solutions available for the solo and small firm that provide reliable and secure network connections. Linksys continues to be a very popular manufacturer of wireless networking devices for residential users and small to medium-sized businesses. The Linksys EA3500 N750 Dual-Band Smart Wi-Fi Wireless Router is an all-in-one internet-sharing router with a four-port switch. Although this router can be used to connect your local computer network to the internet, it should be implemented as a wireless access point only in coordination with another firewall/IDS/IPS device. The 802.11n wireless standard protocol is used by this device and offers data transmission speeds up to 300 Mbps. This standard is about six times as fast as the 802.11g standard, which offered data transmission speeds up to 54 Mbps. One of the benefits of the 802.11n standard is that it is backward compatible with all 802.11b/g devices. This router supports the latest wireless security encryption standards, such as WPA2, to keep your data communications secure. The Linksys EA3500 N750 Dual-Band Smart Wi-Fi Wireless Router can be purchased online from the Linksys website (store.linksys.com) or from your local electronics retailer for around $70.

Wireless device manufacturers continue their push to get consumers to purchase their 802.11ac wireless products. The 802.11ac standard has been approved since early 2014, so it's fine to purchase and use these products. Wireless networks that use the 802.11ac standard will see an improvement in connection speeds and range beyond previous 802.11 standard connections. To use the new standard, all wireless devices will have to be 802.11ac compatible; otherwise, the wireless network will operate using only the same standard as the "oldest" wireless device on your network. Further, to get transmission speeds as fast as advertised, you'll have to be relatively close to the access point, and only a limited number of devices can be connected and using the wireless network at the same time.

If you work in a large office space, in a building with a lot of brick or mesh metal wiring embedded within the walls, or in a cubicle next to a microwave, you can purchase a piece of hardware to extend or improve the wireless signal strength in your office. These wireless range extenders can cost as little as $25. Realistically, you should plan to spend somewhere between $50 and $100 for a range extender, which can be purchased online.

CHAPTER NINE

Smartphones

Smartphones remain the number one tech accessory among lawyers. Smartphones are like laptops—able to perform almost every function a laptop can, and in some instances, more—but at a fraction of the size. Because smartphones have so many capabilities, lawyers in firms of all sizes tend to view them as a necessity—a device they can no longer live or go anywhere without. Smartphones are computers in and of themselves, with increasing functionality, and in some cases, they are more important to a lawyer than a computer system. And sadly, they have become a kind of crack, with many lawyers seriously addicted to them and unable to disengage from technology, risking their health and relationships. That aside . . .

Among business users and especially lawyers, the smartphone debate has evolved into major warfare. Since its introduction and with its growing popularity, the Apple iPhone has grabbed the largest share of the lawyer market, and that is particularly true for solo and small firm lawyers.

According to the American Bar Association's 2017 Legal Technology Survey, Apple's iPhone continues to be the dominant phone used by attorneys and smartphones continue to be the most used computing device, followed by the desktop computer. Here is the breakdown of mobile phones used by attorneys:

- Apple iPhone: 75 percent
- Google Android: 23 percent
- BlackBerry: 2 percent
- Windows Mobile: 1 percent
- Don't Know: 1 percent

These numbers have not really changed since last year's report and have been stable for the past five years. Here are a few summary points regarding the findings:

- There are only two major players in the smartphone market, iPhone and Android.

- iPhone's usage increased slightly to 75 percent, while Android's usage stayed flat at 23 percent.
- Windows Mobile and BlackBerry devices are non-factors.

Both the Android and the iPhone continue to split the market share at an almost 98 percent combined share of the market. The BlackBerry is no longer used—it has become all but nonexistent in the United States, and the same is true of the Windows Mobile phone. BlackBerry (the name of the device and the company name) may have been lulled into inaction by its early success, but the hot technology continues clearly to belong to Androids and iPhones. Because BlackBerry is a Canadian company, Canada continues to keep it on life support. Microsoft is no different. Microsoft sold its feature phone business to a Foxconn subsidiary and is licensing the Nokia name for handsets back to Nokia. Amid the plummeting sale of Lumia devices this past year, Microsoft is essentially done in the phone business and is no longer offering support for Windows on a mobile device.

A key functional requirement for any smartphone is the ability to synchronize data with your computer or server. Email synchronization is at the top of all lawyers' lists, followed closely by calendar synchronization. The Windows Phone 8 and 8.1, Windows Phone 10, iPhone, and Android phones synchronize with Microsoft Exchange Servers via ActiveSync. This doesn't require any special hardware or software because the function is built into Exchange. However, there are some limitations, such as the inability to synchronize natively with Public Folders over the air. You may have to purchase third-party products to get all of the features you need for over-the-air (OTA) synchronization of Public Folder items such as Calendar Items, Contact Items, InfoPath Form Items, Journal Items, Mail and Post Items, Note Items, and Task Items. For this task, we use and recommend CodeTwo Exchange Sync (http://www.codetwo.com/exchange-folder-sync/). The cost to purchase and install this product will vary depending on the type of Exchange server that you have—Small Business Server or Exchange Server Standard/Enterprise—but will generally cost under $800 to get you up and running, plus another couple hundred or so for a year of support, which you will want to renew annually.

Your mailbox will synchronize without any additional software. For those firms that do not host their own email, users can set up their devices to retrieve email directly from their email service provider.

iPhone

Our continuing recommendation for lawyers is to use an Android mobile device. While iPhone security has gotten better, significantly so, there still are some issues—and the iPhones hold a lot more data than other phones. Those of us in the digital forensics world call them "evidence-rich." Apple just released three new models as we are writing this book and the security of those devices is unknown, although we expect it to be another improvement over previous models as has been historically true.

The new flagship iPhone comes in three flavors, the iPhone XR, XS, and XS Max running iOS 12. The iPhone XS is 5.8 inches long; the iPhone XR is 6.1 inches long; the iPhone XS Max is a whopping 6.5 inches long, which is huge for a smartphone. It is almost as if you are holding an iPad Mini next to your head—too large for our taste. Each of the newly released iPhone models are water-resistant, hold a longer battery life, and have dual-SIM and wireless charging capabilities.

What is the difference between the three models released concurrently? Besides the price, the iPhone XS Max comes with a dramatically larger Super Retina Display with greater resolution than the XR model. These three models use Face ID facial recognition for user authentication and shoot and record 4K video. All of these devices did retain the Lightening port, but now can charge wirelessly. The iPhone XR starts at $749, XS at $999, and SX Max at $1,099 for the 64 GB models.

The lack of a standard headphone jack will forever annoy some users because the device uses the Lightning port instead and comes with EarPods with Lightning Connector. You do have the option to purchase wireless AirPods for a whopping $159 instead of using the Lightning Connector EarPods. Supposedly, the AirPods will last five hours on a single charge, but Apple's history of poor battery life with iPhones makes us skeptical.

The new iOS 12 includes performance increases in reducing the amount of time the camera, keyboard display and apps load on the mobile device. Users may now FaceTime with up to 32 people at once, with the tile of the person speaking getting larger automatically so it is easy to track the conversation. One of the more important features in the era of too much connectivity is Screen Time, which allows users and parents the ability to restrict device and app usage on a granular level. It will also tell you how much time you spend actively on the phone during a specific period and can email reports, which may be beneficial for lawyers looking for a reason to disconnect!

The government has been making the same complaints about iPhone and Android encryption since the release of the Android Lollipop operating system in 2014. The encryption of data on these mobile devices continues to be an obstacle to the National Security Agency (and others) from being able to access the encrypted contents of these devices in a timely fashion, potentially hampering or slowing down their investigations. Recently, with the release and availability of the GrayKey device and Cellebrite's Advanced Unlocking Services geared towards Law Enforcement, most iPhone devices running up to iOS 11 can be unlocked without knowing the PIN or passphrase. For a sense of cost, the GrayKey device comes in two flavors—a $15,000-a-year license option (up to 300 unlocks) and $30,000 option, which comes with unlimited unlocks. As we go to print, it appears that with the release of iOS 12.1, Apple has successfully defeated GrayKey's ability to bypass the lock code for the present time.

Not much has changed in the security model of Apple's iPhone devices. There still are security problems with the current generation of the devices. Like every previous version of iOS, a jailbreak for iOS 12 has already emerged.

Because we know so many lawyers will (and do) ignore our advice, here is what we recommend if you must use an iPhone:

- Only use the iPhone 8, 8 Plus, X, XR, XS, or XS Max. If you're using any other model, upgrade immediately.
- Upgrade to the latest version of iOS 12, and install updates in a timely fashion.
- Enable a passphrase (not the default six-digit PIN) on the device and only use a passphrase to unlock the phone.
- Enable device wiping upon a set number of unsuccessful logon attempts.

Specific to iOS 12, there are some additional security measures that you should enable when setting up the device. One of first things you must do is turn on automatic iOS updating. This will allow your device to receive fixes for security issues in between major version updates. Apple has enabled USB restricted mode by default in iOS 12, which is believed to prevent GrayShift and Cellebrite from bypassing the iOS lock screen. You can check the setting by going to Settings—Touch ID (Face ID) & Passcode and make sure USB Accessories toggle is set to off.

We strongly recommend that you configure a strong lock code and not the default six-digit PIN. Even though the FBI is reported to have paid approximately $1.3 million to access the San Bernardino iPhone 5c, security researchers have been able to "mirror" the memory for $100 and brute force every possible PIN. Once the phone wipes, they just restore the memory image and keep trying PINs. We are well aware that our advice is largely ignored here, as the glamour of the iPhone continues to mesmerize the public, including lawyers. It is a very slick phone, but remember that the new ABA Model Rules adopted in 2012 require that you balance the risk of the technology you use against the security of client data!

iCloud

With the introduction of iOS 5 back in 2012, Apple introduced the iCloud service. When enabled and configured, iOS devices use this service to back up information from your local device to the cloud. The iCloud service removes the necessity to connect your iOS device to your computer and either backup or update your device by using iTunes. All of this now takes place wirelessly, over your mobile data connection or your local Wi-Fi network. However, while convenient, there are some serious concerns with data privacy.

Consider that all information from your local device, whether the iPhone or iPad, is being sent to Apple for storage. The information may be encrypted by Apple, but it holds the decryption key and will turn the decrypted data over to law enforcement when the right paperwork is supplied. The 2014 Celebgate scandal, in which nearly 500 private photos of various celebrities were leaked to the public, have highlighted the insecurity and dangers of the iCloud, especially if you want to store your nude selfies (or other sensitive material) on Apple's service. To secure your iCloud account from unauthorized access, users should enable and use two-factor authentication—which was implemented in response to Celebgate. When two-factor authentication is enabled, a password alone is no longer enough to access an account—you will also need the six-digit verification code that's automatically displayed on your trusted devices. Even though Apple can currently decrypt your iCloud data, it has indicated that it plans to change the security design to match the iPhone. This means that data will be able to be decrypted only by end-user-supplied credentials and not by Apple.

For any cloud storage provider, whether iCloud, Dropbox, or some other provider, we always recommend that you encrypt the data prior to using and initiating the service. By following this process, the user holds the decryption key—not the service provider.

For iOS devices, an app like BoxCryptor encrypts the files on your local device before the information is synchronized with the cloud storage provider. BoxCryptor encrypts files on the local device using AES 256–bit and RSA encryption, providing the necessary security to keep your files and information secure. This also allows the user to hold and maintain possession of the decryption key, which is very important. This product used to be free, and still is for personal use, but costs $96 per year for a single-user business license.

Android

During the past few years, many vendors of Android smartphones have continued to release phones designed for business use. They include enhanced security and enterprise management capabilities, like encryption, support for virtual private networks, support for more ActiveSync controls, and remote locking and wiping.

In August 2018, Google released version 9.0 of Android, called Pie. Some of the new features include a new user interface for settings, new screenshot button, updated messaging notifications, lock screen security changes, DNS requests are now made over TLS, and a Wind Down feature that lets users set a specific bedtime that enables Do Not Disturb and turns the entire phone's interface gray to discourage further use.

For those users looking for a smartphone recommendation, we strongly recommend investing in Android phones. We officially made the jump six years ago to the Samsung Galaxy S3 and have not looked back. We have fallen in love with the Samsung Galaxy line of devices and have used many of the models. The Samsung Galaxy S9 and S9+ are the latest available models and are available with 64 GB of internal memory and in six different colors.

Besides the Samsung Galaxy model line, there are many other Android devices to choose from. It may help to choose your cellular provider first and then see what options it has. We've been to many Sprint, Verizon, and AT&T stores—nowadays, they all pretty much have the same models in stock with many more options available online. For an Android, the Samsung Galaxy S9 is our current recommendation.

Text Message Spam Control

On a side note, everyone is familiar with getting spam through email, but how about on the phone? Spam text messages can be costly since most carriers will charge for both text messages sent and received unless you have an unlimited plan. There is no anti-SMS-spam software available to install on cell phones to prevent receiving these messages, but there is a way to block cellular spam, and it's quite simple. The vast majority of spam text messages originates on the internet and does not come from other cell phones. Why? Because spammers don't have to pay anything when using the internet to send the text messages. Most carriers, led by AT&T and Verizon Wireless, offer spam SMS-blocking features. To enable this feature, just log in to your online account manager and the options should be available in your account profile. Most cellular providers allow you to block SMS messages only from certain phone numbers and addresses. What are you waiting for? We've signed up. Here are the websites you can use:

- AT&T (mymessages.wireless.att.com)
- Verizon Wireless (www.verizonwireless.com)
- Sprint (www.sprint.com)
- T-Mobile (www.t-mobile.com)

Security Products

Make sure you pay attention to smartphone updates and security notices, as the number of malware threats targeting smartphones have skyrocketed in 2018. This means applying operating system updates as soon as available from your carrier. Apple users should always be running the latest version of iOS. Basic security measures for any smartphone include strong passwords, passphrases, or PINs; automatic locking after a set period of inactivity; encryption of the phone and storage cards; and remote wiping capability. The good news is that configuring a lock code (PIN, password, etc.) on an iPhone or newer Android device automatically encrypts the contents. Currently, Android devices are the most frequently targeted by malware due to their popularity, open-source operating system, the relatively lawless Android Market, and the availability of apps from multiple sources.

Even with the rising threat of malware, there are some basic steps you can take to protect yourself. First, make sure that when you're downloading an application, you do so only from trusted sources such as Google Play or the App Store. When choosing an application to try or to purchase, be sure to read carefully through the reviews. Also, pay attention to the access permissions that an app requests when you install it, especially on an Android device. Finally, vendors of security software are now offering antivirus and anti-malware products for smartphones. This is software that you should seriously consider purchasing to protect your mobile devices, especially if they contain confidential information, which they most certainly do.

For Android phones, we recommend a security product called Sophos Mobile Security for Android (https://www.sophos.com/en-us/products/free-tools/sophos-mobile-security-free-edition.aspx). Specifically designed for Android, Sophos Mobile Security identifies malicious or potentially unwanted applications that could result in, for example, data theft, data loss, and excessive network usage costs. If your device is lost or stolen, a remote lock or wipe will shield your personal information from prying eyes. iPhone users should also install security software to protect the device. All of the major anti-virus vendors also make products for mobile devices. Sophos is also a good choice for iPhone users.

CHAPTER TEN

Productivity Software

Having worked with many solos and small law firms through the years, we know that lawyers are constantly striving to be more productive and thereby increase their billable time. It's been many years since we've had a support call to install or troubleshoot Corel WordPerfect. Corel is pretty much a nonfactor in the productivity software market.

Microsoft Word is what the business world uses and will continue to use for the foreseeable future. There are alternatives, but they all come with some degree of pain and a large learning curve. There are adherents of WordPerfect who are religious in their fervor and others who are evangelical in their admiration for open-source solutions. Whether you are a fan of Microsoft or not, the reality is that Word is the preferred application of the business world, and your clients will expect you to use it. They will not appreciate any conversion problems that may occur if you are using something else. In this chapter, we detail the latest and greatest releases of productivity software that can help lawyers be more productive.

Microsoft Office

Microsoft has released the newest version of its productivity software, Office 2019, and it is available for purchase as a stand-alone solution. Users need to know that Office 2019 will only run on computers running Windows 10, and will not run on Windows 7 or 8.1. On the Mac side, it will run on the three most-recent versions of macOS (10.12 to 10.14). Microsoft has updated the core apps, Word, Excel, PowerPoint, and Outlook, but the updated features have been available for a while now to Office 365 subscribers. As we write, it is unclear if there will be versions of Office 2019 that contain different products (e.g. Word, OneNote, Skype, etc.) like the current versions of Office 2016. For us, we will continue to use Office 2016 until there is a substantial reason to upgrade. For Office 365 subscribers, it makes sense to upgrade at your convenience, which is what you are paying for after all!

Office 2016, now the predecessor, came out in the fall of 2015. The software was redesigned to make the most of the Windows 8 and 10 operating systems, work with mobile devices, and strongly push Microsoft's cloud services. It works and runs just fine on Microsoft Windows 10, and it is our current choice and recommendation for a productivity suite.

To compete with Google's cloud storage options, Microsoft designed the new version of Office as a service in which applications and files are primarily stored in the cloud and not on your local computer system. This may come as a shock to most traditional Microsoft users, and lawyers should be aware that this type of service may pose ethical issues depending on how and where their information is actually being stored. However, users also have the ability to store documents on their local computer system.

Each of the three editions of Office 2016 includes the core applications of Word, Excel, PowerPoint, and OneNote:

- Home & Student, designed for families and consumers; core applications only; retails for $149.99
- Home & Business, designed for the small business market; provides email hosting, shared calendars, and web conferencing tools; core applications and Outlook; retails for $229.99
- Professional, designed for enterprise customers; provides advanced business and cloud deployment features; core applications plus Outlook, Publisher, and Access; retails for $399.99

If your firm is using Microsoft Office 2010 or older, we highly recommend that you upgrade to Office 2016 at this time. Office 2013 users should be just fine unless you want to take advantage of the collaboration features of Office 2016.

Microsoft, like a lot of companies, is making a very strong push to get users to the cloud and away from local applications. To accomplish this goal, Microsoft, some time back, introduced a software as a service (SaaS) called Office 365, which gives users and companies the option to purchase a subscription (monthly or annually) to use the Microsoft Office applications in the cloud, and in some instances, also includes the ability to install and use the stand-alone versions. As we go to press, it appears that Microsoft is changing the name of the product to Microsoft 365, but we will continue to use Office 365 for this edition of our book because that is what lawyers today know as its name!

The subscription-based Office 365 may not be for everyone, but for a solo or small firm, it at least presents another licensing option—rather than having to shovel out hundreds of dollars per license for the stand-alone versions of the Office 2016 suite. Make no mistake—lawyers are moving to Office 365 in droves. The Business Essentials subscription is entirely cloud-based and costs $5 per user per month ($60 per year), but doesn't include the ability to run Office on a mobile device, such as an iPad, or to install Office on your local computer. This requires you to connect to the internet in order to use Microsoft Office, which is a major downside. The Business subscription costs $8.25 per user per month ($99 per year), but doesn't include email hosting (storing your email with Microsoft), which is different than the Outlook application. This subscription plan does allow you to install the full version of Office on your local computer (including Outlook) and use the Office apps on your tablet or mobile device. Finally, the Business Premium subscription costs $12.50 per month per user ($150 per year), includes Office for tablets, and allows for the installation of Microsoft Office 2016 on up to five computer systems per user ($30/license). For a small firm just starting up that is looking to be mobile, shelling out $12.50 per month for your employees to use Office may be easier to swallow than paying up to $400 per copy of Microsoft Office 2016. It's just another option to consider.

In addition to the Business subscription plans, Microsoft offers several Enterprise plans. The top-level Enterprise plan costs $35 per user per month (annual commitment) and includes features that attorneys will love. As an example, Enterprise E3 includes Compliance and Information Protection, including Legal Hold, Rights Management, and Data Loss Prevention for email and files. There are also e-discovery tools to support compliance. The Enterprise plans can get expensive for some solo and small firm attorneys, but some may feel it's worth the extra money just to get Data Loss Prevention for their email. You can see the features for each edition of Office 365 at https://products.office.com/en-us/business/compare-more-office-365-for-business-plans.

We are seeing a lot of solo and small firms migrating to Office365, and in general, we hear that lawyers are very satisfied with the cost and performance. We want to make sure to recommend Ben Schorr's new book, *Microsoft Office 365 for Lawyers, 2nd edition*, which is available from the ABA web store. Ben's books are remarkable reference tools and always laced with easy-to-read (and often humorous) dialogue.

It should be noted that Microsoft Office 365 includes support for Office 2016 for Macs, which is available for those subscriptions with the ability to install a full version of the Office suite locally on a computer system. One of the other major advantages of Office 365 is the ability for Microsoft to update its applications in "real time," without having to wait to release updates for users to take advantage of new or improved features.

Editing Office documents on tablets (and other mobile devices) has long been a major headache, which could only be overcome by using third-party applications to perform the simplest tasks of opening, editing, and saving documents on the mobile device. Microsoft has released Office for mobile devices, including Office for iPad and Office Mobile for the iPhone, Windows Phone, and Android devices.

Office for iPad has been an app that the legal community has been waiting for and now it is here. This app allows users to edit and create documents, including spreadsheets and presentations. Office for iPad requires a subscription to Office 365; however, Office Mobile is free to download on your Android, iPhone, or Windows Phone. Just remember that an Office 365 subscription is required if you want to edit Office files and not just view them.

For those attorneys who require email encryption (most of you should be using email encryption by now), Microsoft has released a service called Office 365 Message Encryption. This service lets users send encrypted emails to people outside your firm, regardless of the destination (Yahoo, Gmail, Outlook, etc.). Encryption is critical when sending messages that contain personally identifiable information, credit card numbers, medical records, and Social Security numbers, to just name a few types of sensitive information. Office 365 Message Encryption requires Microsoft Azure Rights Management, which costs $2 per user per month. If you have the E3 or E5 subscription of Office 365 Enterprise, Azure Rights Management is included in the cost, so you automatically get email encryption without having to pay the extra $2 per user per month.

Microsoft recently introduced a scoring system for the configuration and set up of its customers Office 365 account, called Secure Score. This scoring system is a metric that is intended to be used by clients to determine how secure their configuration is, allowing Microsoft to provide recommendations for its customers to improve their security posture. We think of it as a credit score for security.

Secure Score gives you a different way of managing your risk. Rather than reacting or responding to security alerts, the Secure Score lets you track and plan incremental improvements over a longer period of time.

The Secure Score does not express an absolute measure of how likely you are to experience a data breach. Rather, it expresses the extent to which you have adopted security controls which can help thwart data breaches. As we always state, no service can offer you a 100 percent guarantee that your data will remain secure.

Secure Score determines what Office 365 services you are using, looks at your configuration and behaviors, and then compares it to a baseline asserted by Microsoft. If your configuration and behaviors are in line with best practices, your score increases, which users can track over time. More importantly, users are able to determine what things they can implement to strengthen the protection of data stored within Office 365.

While some of the changes to Office 365 occur behind the scenes, like auditing or reviewing reports weekly, others are more time consuming and noticeable to users when implemented, like enabling Multi-Factor Authentication (MFA) or implementing a Mobile Device Manager (MDM).

Microsoft takes the guesswork out of achieving these security-minded goals by providing a checklist of tasks and instructions on how to complete those tasks. Once implemented, the secure score will go up. The default score after just implementing Office 365 is 27 and the highest score you can achieve is 450. We recommend that clients aim to get above a score of 250, which will help to increase the security of data stored within Office 365 and reduce the potential risk of a data breach occurring. As we write, there are changes being made to Secure Score which may impact the math above, so make sure you visit Microsoft's site (https://docs.microsoft.com/en-us/office 365/securitycompliance/office-365-secure-score) to get the latest information. There is now a combined Secure Score for Microsoft Windows and Microsoft Office. Because these changes are moving quickly, make sure you check the current status.

Some of the means to increase the Secure Score include adding additional security features to your Office 365 account. Microsoft charges $1.40 per user per month for Multi-Factor Authentication, $6.00 per user per month for the Mobile Device Manager (MDM) called InTune, and Advanced Threat Protection (ATP) costs $2.00 per user per month. These are just some of the larger steps firms can take to increase their security posture and Secure Score.

Corel Suite

WordPerfect Office X9 is the most recent version of Corel's Office Suite, and it is available in Standard and Professional editions for the business user. WordPerfect Office X9, the successor to WordPerfect Office X8, became available in May 2018. New features of Corel WordPerfect Office X9 include an enhanced Reveal Codes feature, allowing users to change the color of the space character, open multiple WordPerfect windows at the same time (upgrade from the previous nine-document limit), and offers users the ability to save a file to multiple formats at the same time. Some of the legal features that may be of interest to firms include Bates Numbering capabilities and a Legal toolbar that allows attorneys to create and format pleading papers, generate indexes and tables of contents, and even create a Table of Authorities. The components of WordPerfect Office X9 Standard Edition include

- WordPerfect word processor
- Quattro Pro spreadsheet program
- Presentations slideshow creator
- WordPerfect Lightning digital notebook
- eBook Publisher
- AfterShot 3 photo-editing and management

The Professional Edition also adds:

- Paradox database management system
- Corel Screencap
- Roxio Secure Burn

Corel X9 is available in Standard and Professional editions, but the Standard Edition is best suited for serving solo or small firm needs. Unless a solo or small firm needs a database application, there is no reason for it to invest in the Professional Edition.

One of the touted advantages of WordPerfect over Microsoft Word is the Reveal Codes option, which allows users to manage document formatting with a fine-tooth comb. We are constantly amazed when lawyers mention the reveal code "excuse." Perhaps they are unaware that Word actually has a reveal code type display (and Office has since 2007), where the user can see formatting codes.

Even with the new features included with WordPerfect Office X9, which appear to be lackluster, we still prefer the seamless Microsoft Office 2016. Another concern is the integration of WordPerfect with other software in your practice such as case management and document management. You can see a listing of products that work with WordPerfect at https://www.wordperfect.com/us/pages/4500028.html. Corel used to price the software suite at a much reduced cost when compared to Microsoft Office, particularly for business-friendly packages, but that hasn't been the case for many years. Full license and upgrade costs for the two editions are below.

Edition	Full License Cost	Upgrade Cost
Standard Edition	$249.00	$159.99
Professional Edition	$399.00	$259.99

Although we don't recommend it, users who don't need the extensive features of WordPerfect or Microsoft Office might opt to use a product such as LibreOffice, which is free.

LibreOffice

LibreOffice has become the open-source office suite replacement for OpenOffice, which is now all but defunct. LibreOffice forked from OpenOffice.org in 2010, and is developed around the ODF format, just like OpenOffice was.

LibreOffice also supports the file formats of most other major office suites, including Microsoft Office.

LibreOffice includes the same six applications as Open Office—Writer, Calc, Impress, Draw, Math, and Base. LibreOffice is supported on Windows, Linux, and Apple computers, and released a viewer application for Android devices with basic editing capabilities in the spring of 2015.

If you're looking at trying one of the open-source office suites, LibreOffice would be the one to use. You can download the latest version of the free suite, 6.1.1, from www.libreoffice.org. LibreOffice uses a time-based release schedule for major updates, which ends up releasing one every four to eight months—so make sure you check for updates periodically.

Adobe Acrobat

Adobe Acrobat, a family of application software developed by Adobe Systems, uses Portable Document Format (PDF) as its native file format. The PDF specification was originally a proprietary format but is now a published and approved ISO standard. The latest version of Adobe Acrobat (DC) includes Adobe Document Cloud services and is notably different from previous versions. Document Cloud allows users to create, review, approve, and sign documents from any desktop or mobile device. Since the program is integrated for the cloud, a user can begin working on a document on one device and then continue editing it on another. Adobe Acrobat PDF files can easily be created or edited from a mobile device, such as an Apple iPad. The latest update added support for SharePoint-based reviews, including participants using Microsoft Office 2016 (Windows and Macs).

Adobe Acrobat DC allows users to convert, combine, and export PDFs easier than ever. The Export PDF to Word feature has been enhanced, hopefully fixing all of the formatting problems previously experienced when attempting to accomplish this task. The Pro DC version contains all of the features that attorneys love such as Bates numbering and redaction capabilities. Users may also secure their PDFs with passwords using 128-bit or 256-bit AES encryption and permission controls to protect document viewing, printing, and modifications.

Adobe Acrobat DC is offered in a subscription model only. A stand-alone solution (named after the year, 2017) is available, without the cloud-based integration. The Acrobat DC subscriptions start at $12.99 per month per user for the Standard plan, which includes the desktop version of the Acrobat 2017 software as well as the cloud-integration and mobile features. Subscribers will also get 20 GBs of cloud storage with their plan.

Users can still opt for the stand-alone version of the Adobe Acrobat Pro 2017 software at a cost of $449 for the full version of Acrobat Pro 2017 or $299 for the full version of Acrobat Standard 2017. The upgrade versions of these products are priced much lower than the full versions, allowing for users of Acrobat X and XI to upgrade at a fraction of the cost. The cost to upgrade to Acrobat Pro 2017 is $199, and the cost to upgrade to Acrobat Standard 2017 is $139. This product is supported on Windows 10 as well as the latest version of Mac OS X. To purchase the stand-alone versions, users will have to go to Adobe's online webstore (https://www.adobe.com/products/catalog.html?) and "filter the apps by type" to Desktop, and then will be presented with the option to purchase the Pro or Standard version of Acrobat, without a subscription.

Adobe has recently released an update to Acrobat DC that enhances the Compare Documents tool, as well as allows users to digitally sign, certify, and verify documents with a Certificate ID. The Compare Documents tool allows users to compare the contents of two documents and highlight the differences between the two, including text, images, annotations, and formatting. Adobe has made it easier to follow prompts to configure a digital ID and add it to a document, allowing the document to be digitally signed.

Adobe DC has now included the ability to capture a user's signature with a mobile device and to collect e-signatures from other users and track responses in real time. The ability to collect and sign documents online from a mobile device is becoming increasingly popular among attorneys.

As we were performing our final edits for this book, Adobe announced that Acrobat DC now includes the robust e-sign solution Adobe Sign for no additional charge. Adobe Sign integrates with Microsoft Office 365, so users can create and send contracts for signature and monitor their status in Word, PowerPoint or Outlook. Adobe has also integrated this product with Microsoft Dynamics 365, SharePoint and OneDrive.

This product is very simple for each party to use, just like sending an email. The creator enters the signers' email address, along with the fields to collect e-signatures and other information. Then they hit Send—it's that easy. Recipients simply click a link and sign the document in a browser on their computer or mobile device. The recipient doesn't need to download any application or create any account. The creator is notified as soon as the document is viewed or signed, and reminders can be sent to keep the document signing process moving forward. For more guidance on how to effectively use Adobe Acrobat DC, we recommend that you purchase *The Ultimate Guide to Adobe Acrobat DC* authored by Dan Siegel and Pamela Myers from the ABA bookstore.

Power PDF

For those users who are looking for an alternative to Adobe Acrobat, our recommendation is to use Power PDF Advanced 3 by Nuance. It is certainly a worthy alternative and is only one-third of the retail cost of Acrobat Pro. Power PDF Advanced has Bates stamping support to create custom profiles for stamping information into headers and footers. There's also an assistant function to convert legal pleadings into PDFs with stamp and line numbering options. Redaction ability is included too. Users may also secure their PDFs with passwords using 128-bit or 256-bit AES encryption and permission controls to protect document viewing, printing, and modifications. The program also integrates with cloud storage providers, allowing users to save their PDFs directly in the cloud. Some of the new features included in the latest version are the ability to covert a PDF file to Office documents, Microsoft Windows 10 touch-enabled input, and integration via Ribbon into Microsoft Office 2016 products. Documents can integrate with DocuSign, for capturing secure electronic signatures. Users can now collaborate, working on the same document in real-time with multiple people on the same network.

There are many other features available with Power PDF Advanced 3. Suffice it to say that it has the majority of features present in Acrobat Pro that any attorney would find valuable. The cost of a license for $179 is attractive as well. Make sure you take advantage of the 30-day trial to determine if it will meet your needs. It should be noted that this product is Windows 10 compatible.

OCR Software

Optical character recognition (OCR) software translates graphical images into editable text. This capability is used most commonly to edit a scanned document or image. It's widely used in law firms to convert scanned paper documents in a case file to searchable electronic files. OCR software will translate the image to text, such as a Microsoft Word document, which can be edited.

OmniPage Ultimate, by Nuance Communications, Inc., is an OCR software product enabling the conversion of paper documents and TIFF files to a text-based format for amending as needed with prominent business communications software. OmniPage Ultimate can convert scanned images to Microsoft Word, Excel, PowerPoint, Corel WordPerfect, email, HTML, and even to the Amazon Kindle format. The program generates a formatted text document that preserves the layout and format, character, font, and style of the scanned image. This software boasts a 50 percent greater accuracy rate than its competitors when converting, and the updated recognition dictionaries for financial, legal, and medical specialties allow for legal-specific word recognition, which means that you will spend less time editing your legal documents. This software can also process, edit, and recognize over 120 languages—a great feature for those firms with a global presence.

OmniPage supports data capture from a digital camera. The software can "read" a digital photograph, which may come in handy for lawyers who use photographs as exhibits. This software is the first OCR application designed for the multicore-processor computer, taking advantage of hyperthreading to increase the conversion speed of documents. It was also the first OCR software to support Microsoft Office 2007/2010 native formats. When converting legal documents, OmniPage now has a greater ability to recognize formatting such as line numbers, Bates stamps, signatures, and more.

Other new OmniPage Ultimate features worth mentioning include the ability to convert a scanned document into a readable format and send it to an Amazon Kindle, a "one click" toolbar in the Microsoft Office Suite that allows for document conversion with a simple click, and a faster load time than previous versions.

The DocuDirect feature can automatically send converted files to a predefined destination, multiple destinations, or on-demand to anyone. It can also watch a shared folder and automatically send converted files into the most appropriate workflow.

Also new in the latest version of OmniPage is the eDiscovery Assistant for searchable PDFs. The eDiscovery Assistant provides the ability to convert a single PDF or batches of PDFs of all types into searchable documents without having to open PDF files one by one, giving the user greater flexibility when applying an OCR process to an entire group of documents.

As more and more firms look to use the features the internet cloud provides, so do vendors. OmniPage includes the Nuance Cloud Connector application, which integrates with Evernote, Dropbox, OneDrive, and Google Drive, allowing users to scan and save their documents to the cloud.

OmniPage Ultimate can be purchased and downloaded online directly from Nuance's website (www.nuance.com) for $499.99 for the full version and $199.99 for the upgrade version.

Adobe Acrobat includes an OCR engine too and the ability to batch OCR documents—and not just one at a time. We recommend purchasing Adobe Acrobat or Power PDF first to see if it meets your OCR needs before expending funds on another specialized product like OmniPage.

Voice Recognition Software

Arguably one of the biggest recent advances in productivity software is the continuing refinement of voice recognition software. Dragon Naturally Speaking by Nuance (www.nuance.com) has made voice recognition software a respectable addition to your productivity arsenal. Many solo and small firm lawyers are now using Dragon as their primary composition tool. This is especially valuable for those who are not very accurate or fast typists. It takes only a short time to train Dragon to your voice, and its accuracy is astonishing. Nuance claims that the latest version is up to 24 percent more accurate than the previous version, which is just incredible given how accurate the previous version of this product was.

Dragon can be used to compose email messages, draft documents in your word processor, and even launch software applications without touching the keyboard or mouse. The software now allows users to search the web and their computers through the use of voice shortcuts.

Along with new formatting and editing commands, the latest version also provides users with the ability to post to Facebook and Twitter by voice and even allows users to use their iPhone or iPad as a wireless microphone, untethering them from their computer.

Some of the new features include

- Support for Windows 10 touchscreen PCs
- Support for WordPerfect X9 and Skype for Business
- Accuracy is improved over the previous version—the new version continues to "learn" your voice and becomes more accurate the more you use the product
- The software now learns words and phrases you use most
- Multicore processors provide faster performance
- Go hands free and headset free—the software now offers multiple microphone options, including those built into the latest laptops, so that you can type even less and not have to use a headset
- Dictate notes and ideas on the go and transcribe the audio files back at your computer

This is a great tool and is used by many individuals with disabilities. But make no mistake—this is a mainstream product, and the able-bodied are moving to this technology in hordes!

Dragon Naturally Speaking comes in several versions. We recommend using the Legal or Professional version 15 if you can afford it. The Legal version contains vocabulary specific to the legal profession and carries a price tag of $500. The Professional version is a higher-end package that allows for roaming user profiles and allows multiple custom dictionaries. The Professional Individual version costs $300 and may be purchased from many webstores or directly from the Nuance site. Users must purchase Dragon Naturally Speaking on a per-user basis. You can install and run it on multiple computers, but you need a license for each user's voice file.

The most important tip about using voice recognition software is to proof any output from Dragon. The speech-to-text is very good, and it "learns" and improves with time, but it's not perfect. Make sure you proofread your documents, especially those that may be submitted to a court.

If you use Dragon on multiple computers, make sure you know how to move your voice files among machines. This will save on the "retraining" time when you use several computers. The process is most appropriate for those lawyers who use a computer at home and one at the office. Moving the voice files between the machines allows you to take advantage of the aggregate training time instead of each machine "learning" on its own.

A key component to the success of voice recognition is the use of a good quality USB microphone headset. We have had great success using a Plantronics 510 headset/microphone system, but they are no longer manufactured. The Plantronics Blackwire 720 Series is available for $149.95 from the Plantronics website (www.plantronics.com) and should be an excellent replacement for the older 510 model. The lightweight headphones with noise-canceling microphone connect to your computer using a standard USB or Bluetooth connection. We recommend the USB connection as Bluetooth wireless is more susceptible to audio errors. The wideband acoustic echo cancellation feature captures a broad range of voice signals for calls that are clearer and more natural sounding, perfect for use with Skype. The smart sensor technology lets you answer calls simply by putting on the headset or pause mobile device media playback by taking it off. This pair of headphones also allows for dual connectivity between your computer and mobile phone, allowing users to take phone calls while using their computer without the need to take off the headset.

CHAPTER ELEVEN

Security Software

Combined with network firewalls and IDS/IPS (intrusion detection system/intrusion prevention system) devices, security software provides another line of protection in the defense-in-depth information security strategy against malware, including viruses, Trojan horses, ransomware, and other external forces. The defense-in-depth approach to securing your network is the best way to keep your systems safe from both internal and external threats. These threats can be extremely harmful to a law firm network and very costly to remove once an infection has occurred, assuming you've been able to identify that a breach or infection has taken place. Even in a solo or small firm network, your client data is of the utmost importance, and securing your computers, servers, smartphones, and information should be taken very seriously. The top security protection suites providing antivirus, antispyware, and antispam protection for stand-alone computers, networks, and mobile devices are discussed below, with recommendations regarding the setup and configuration of the software.

In previous editions of this chapter we recommended the usage of Kaspersky security products. Given the uncertain world that we live in and the order by the U.S. Government that directed federal agencies to remove the security suite from its computers, we look at other alternatives below. We used to run Kaspersky on our own computers and servers but we no longer do that. We made the decision to switch reluctantly because Kaspersky security products have always served us well and always score high in independent testing, but the world situation is so destabilized that we became concerned about the optics of dealing with a Russian company.

Security Suites for Individual Computers

The software recommendations described in this section are primarily for the computers and laptops of solo practitioners and the home computers that attorneys may use.

We do not recommend stand-alone products for targeted protection, such as antivirus protection. This type of software is not sufficient today to keep your systems protected. The internet security suites are the only way to go, where you get much more functionality, protection and many more features for your computer at a much more affordable price.

Solos and small firms should definitely consider acquiring a single integrated product to deal with spam, viruses, and malware. Norton's security suite is a top seller for the single computer market. It is highly rated and does a credible job in protecting your computer. However, we don't recommend purchasing Norton for several reasons. It gets average ratings for ease of use, and threat blocking is not on par with the top rated products. We've also found that it may be difficult to uninstall. Norton, along with McAfee, tend to be a heavier load on computer processing versus its competition, although not as bad as versions from several years ago.

For those users who want to avoid the problems that may be caused by Norton and McAfee, we recommend using Webroot SecureAnywhere Internet Security Plus, especially if you like your security suites to be hassle-free. This product contains firewall, antivirus, antispyware, rootkit detection, antispam protection, and much more. This license allows users to install the product on up to three devices, including computers (even Macs) and mobile devices.

The firewall included with this software provides two-way protection, scanning both incoming and outgoing network traffic, effectively blocking any hacker attacks against your system. The automatic exploit protection engine watches program behavior and aims to block zero-day vulnerabilities in the most commonly used software. The anti-phishing engine and URL advisor will keep you safe from driveby malware while you browse the internet, and the anti-banner blocks annoying banners and other advertisements on web pages. This product even comes with webcam protection technology that stops criminals from using your own webcam to spy on you, although we still recommend using electrical tape to cover the webcam. We absolutely do that ourselves. Some of the new features include keeping other applications on your system up to date as updates are available, and as well as providing users with an interface to remove/uninstall software from their computer system.

The mobile application works with both Android and Apple devices and requires Android operating system 4.4 or higher and iOS 10.0 or later. The application allows users to remotely locate, lock or wipe their lost device. This security application will scan other apps for malware and viruses, protects your personal data and identifies and offers continuous protection without battery drain.

Webroot is available directly from its website (www.webroot.com) for $44.99 per year for up to three devices. This is an excellent choice for the small firm environment, and it is Windows 10 compatible.

Enterprise Versions

Enterprise versions of integrated security solutions are designed for small, medium, and large computer networks, and the software administration is performed from the server or centralized console rather than on each individual computer system. The client software is installed or pushed from the central server to the local workstations with little or no effort. The server supplies the clients with program and definition updates and provides an interface to centrally manage all clients from a single console. Of course, enterprise licenses are a little bit more costly than purchasing a single license, but not by much. Even with the slight increase in cost for an enterprise license, you'll more than make up for it on the money you will not have to pay your IT consultant to manage and support the product.

Integrated Security Solutions

Webroot's SecureAnywhere Business Endpoint Protection is the firm's security offering for small, medium and large-sized organizations. It offers all of the same features described in the Internet Security Plus above, plus much more. This product is compatible with Windows and Mac computer systems and servers. It also supports VMware vSphere, Citrix XenDesktop, Hyper-V, and Virtual Box virtualized environments.

This product provides protection from threats such as viruses, Trojans, worms, keyloggers, malware, rootkits, bots, and so on. This is now the standard that we are seeing in the security product market. Former providers of antivirus software are providing protection from spyware and other malware, offering a more complete security solution to their business customers and all but eliminating the need for multiple applications to protect your systems from viruses and malware. This software provides realtime protection by scanning all files that are opened and quarantining infected files. The application can scan specified areas of the file system based on preconfigured, scheduled scans or on demand from the administrator. The scanning of critical system areas, such as running processes and start-up objects, helps prevent malicious code from launching, and the ability to scan inside compound files provides an extra layer of protection.

This software focuses on protecting your systems from different vectors such as threats across email, browsers, files, URLs, ads, apps and more in realtime.

Webroot's product is a scalable security solution, allowing administrators to manage the configuration and software through the online management portal. This software can exist and run alongside other security software, which is a great feature when running other tools such as Malwarebytes or Windows Defender. Definition updates are centrally managed and pushed out to all of the clients within your organization, eliminating the need to manually force updates on your endpoints.

Webroot's SecureAnywhere Business Endpoint Protection, similar to other integrated security solutions, scans not only for viruses but also for other threats and malicious programs, such as spyware and keyloggers. In most instances, this solution can serve multiple functions. By using an integrated solution that is capable of handling both antivirus and antispyware protection, we have one less product to purchase and renew on a yearly basis. The product also allows for different configuration settings depending on the type of network to which the computer system is currently connected, similar to the way Microsoft Windows 8 and 10 handle the different firewall settings.

As the security of smartphones is brought to the public's attention, more vendors are integrating smartphone security with their products. Webroot is no different. SecureAnywhere Business Mobile Protection protects smartphones from data leaks, malware, and viruses, and it also allows an administrator to lock and wipe the device remotely should it be misplaced, stolen, or lost. Some of the additional key features include the ability to enforce company policies such as requiring employees to use a lock passcode to protect sensitive information and encrypt the mobile device.

Business Mobile Protection runs on Android and Apple Mobile devices, running Android operating system 4.0 or higher and Apple's iOS 9.0 and higher. This add-on integrates mobile device protection within the same online endpoint management console used to administer servers and desktops.

There is a five-license minimum purchase for Webroot SecureAnywhere Business Endpoint Protection and Mobile Protection. Cost for the product begins at $45.00 per license per year (both Mobile and Endpoint protection) and includes technical support and upgrades for a year. This product is Windows 10 compatible. Webroot is priced much lower per license than its competition and is an affordable, complete security solution that is rapidly taking over the market. This software product is offered for purchase with a one-year subscription and users also have the option for a free-trial. Licenses can be obtained directly from Webroot's website (www.webroot.com) or from any authorized reseller.

Antispam Protection

For an integrated email security solution, we use (and recommend) Mimecast and love it. However, Mimecast has raised the monthly minimum cost spend for licensing which effectively outprices it from the solo and small firm market. Below, we continue to discuss Mimecast as well as a new competitor on the market, Proofpoint.

Mimecast

Mimecast's email security solution provides an alternative service for email antispam and antivirus without any of the headaches that come with other products, including the products you actually need to install and run on your email server. Note that your email flow will be rerouted so that it goes through Mimecast servers before being delivered to your mail server or email client. You can purchase the Mimecast service directly from the vendor or through a reseller partner.

Mimecast provides three base bundles for email security. S1 is the base security offering and includes basic defenses for malware attacks, social engineering attacks, spam protection, quarantine management and a 30 day rolling archive. The next level is the M2 bundle, which includes all of the features of S1 and adds a 100 percent SLA (Service Level Agreement) backup email uptime and increases the archive to 58 days instead of 30. The third option is the M2A bundle, which has all of the S1 and M2 features and adds unlimited archiving, e-discovery tools and perpetual retention (99 years).

One of the features or add-ins that we subscribe to includes the Large File Send add-on, which allows us to send and receive files up to 2 GB safely without affecting system performance. The Large File Send is integrated with Microsoft Outlook and allows files to be attached directly from the email message window. Large File Send allows senders to encrypt the attachment and provide access keys for users to input in order to download the attachment. Custom expiration dates can be configured and used, setting an expiration date when the attachment is no longer available to the recipient. The authors find themselves using this file sharing add-on more frequently than the alternatives, such as Dropbox. It is simply easier, more secure and provides confirmation of attachment access. It works by "chopping up" the file into smaller segments that are below normal attachment restrictions. Each segment is sent separately to the Mimecast servers where it is reassembled. The user gets a link to download the large file attachment.

Another optional add-on is Secure Messaging, which provides the ability to confidently share sensitive information with external parties via email. It is encrypted messaging via a closed circuit messaging portal. The third and final option (only available with the M2A bundle) is Archive Power Tools, which provides the following functions:

- Replicated Folder Structure & Message Content Stubbing
- User Retention/Folder Based Retention
- Read only view of Calendar Items in Mimecast Personal Portal

Mimecast's solution provides a web-based interface to manage the quarantine, where spam messages are held. Users receive a quarantine message in which they are provided with a summary of the email messages quarantined throughout the day. We have configured notifications of quarantined messages to occur at 8 a.m., 12 noon, and 5 p.m.—three times throughout the work day. From this message, a user can choose to release a quarantined message with just a simple click of the mouse. A user can also "permit" a sender, effectively whitelisting them. Keep in mind that a user can always click on the Mimecast toolbar within Microsoft Outlook to view the current state of the quarantine.

Mimecast also has a "mail bag" feature included with the M2 and M2A bundles. This feature spools your email in the event you lose your internet connection or your email server goes down. Once your connection or server comes back up, Mimecast will synchronize the email that it held and processed during the outage, which means you won't lose any email even if your server goes down for a period of time. Even while your server is down, you can access your email from the web portal or directly through Outlook by activating Continuity Mode, which essentially connects Outlook to the Mimecast servers. In other words, you will not be without email even when your server goes down. Some may think that is a curse rather than a benefit, so we'll let you choose.

Mimecast has a very good reputation for quality service, and clients seem to be very happy with it. Since we started using this product a few years ago, most of our clients have switched as well (now that Postini and McAfee's antispam services are defunct), and the feedback continues to be excellent. You may need to tweak the default rules a bit upon initial installation since Mimecast is pretty aggressive in blocking messages. As an example, email notifications from our credit card payment processor were getting blocked and we were not receiving copies of receipts—which caused a lot of headaches, but we were able to fix all of the problems we identified. Modifying the spam rules is easy, but your administrator should take on this task if needed.

Mimecast provides 24/7 technical support; automatic maintenance and upgrades; and a monthly, annual, or multiyear subscription. This product can be purchased directly from Mimecast (www.mimecast.com). You'll have to request a quote directly from Mimecast, and pricing is dependent on the features selected and number of licenses. The more users, the lower the costs. We feel that you are better off purchasing the service through a Mimecast reseller. They will be able to provide and maintain the service for you. If you go directly through Mimecast, you'll have to maintain your own environment, which is very complicated, but powerful. In addition, we highly recommend the Secure Messaging, Large File Send, and Targeted Threat Protection add-on services. You should be able to get the message security and the recommended add-ons for around $20 per user per month.

As we mentioned earlier, Proofpoint is a less-costly alternative to Mimecast, especially with those firms that only require a few licenses.

Proofpoint

Proofpoint offers similar features as Mimecast and is available for firms to subscribe to without any contract term, which is nice. The Essentials for Small Businesses product offers enterprise-level security that includes spam and phishing detection, analysis of URLs and attachments, social media protection and policy-enforced encryption and data loss prevention. The cloud-based platform allows administrators to access and manage all account settings from a single, secure platform. There are also Continuity and Archive options available, depending on the subscription package your firm selects. Subscriptions are offered in the following classes: Essentials Beginner, Essentials Business, Essentials Advanced and Essentials Professional. Differences between the subscription packages can be found on Proofpoint's website at https://www.proofpoint.com/sites/default/files/essentials_overview_en_v1.pdf and the costs start at $1.50 per user per month for the Essentials Beginner subscription package.

Ransomware Protection

Over the past few years, we have seen many law firms affected by a type of malware called ransomware. Some of the ransomware that we have come across over the last year include variants of CryptoLocker and CryptoWall. Ransomware is a type of malware that restricts access to a computer system and demands that the user pay a ransom to the operators of the malware to remove that restriction—in short, the malware encrypts the user files on a computer system, making them inaccessible. For a fee, the files can be decrypted. It should be noted that we do not recommend paying any ransom, as there is no guarantee that the decryption key will be turned over upon receipt of payment—and, according to the FBI, it is now true that less than 50 percent of those who pay the ransom receive the decryption key. That being said, even the FBI acknowledges that folks have to make their own decision about paying up. To protect against ransomware, we recommend user training, the use of security software, and a well-configured backup solution.

Ransomware continues to be successful in bypassing some security solutions, such as those listed above. One of the reasons for this is the malware's ability to change, and in most instances, it is actually installed by a user with administrative privileges over his local computer. This software has been documented primarily to infect a user's computer through the inadvertent clicking of links embedded within a spam/phishing email or in attachments to such an email. It is now even finding its way onto mobile devices, with ransomware designed to specifically target these platforms.

However, there are steps a firm can take to protect its systems from ransomware. First, make sure your environment is updated on a regular basis. Install operating patches as vendors make them available. In addition, make sure your security software is up to date and configured properly for doing regular scans and actively monitoring your users' computers. Many security solutions have definitions to catch and prevent older versions or variants of ransomware, so it's important to keep these programs running as recommended.

Second, we recommend a product called CryptoPrevent to assist in the blocking and prevention of this malware. CryptoPrevent was designed to protect systems from CryptoLocker and has grown to protect computers against other malware that utilizes the same infection tactics and launch point locations. CryptoPrevent can be downloaded and purchased from the vendor's website at https://www.d7xtech.com/cryptoprevent-malware-prevention for $15 per license per year. This program updates itself automatically as new definitions and signatures are released by the vendor, and it is a product that we have recommended and installed on many of our clients' computer systems.

Third, which may be the most controversial among your employees, is to limit user security permissions by following the Principle of Least Privilege. This requires employees to no longer be configured as "Administrators" of their local computers. Most employees can perform their job function with user accounts set to the "User" or "Power User" security permissions level. In most circumstances, you don't need your receptionist, paralegal, or partner operating as an "Administrator." Why is this such an issue? When a user clicks on a hyperlink or opens up an attachment that they shouldn't have (and we know they will!), malware (ransomware) will be installed with the same security permissions that the current user account has. This can provide the ransomware with Administrator privileges (in most cases), allowing the malware to run and propagate without issue. If malware is going to be installed by users, it would be much better to limit the security permissions it inherits to User, which may drastically reduce its effectiveness and the damage incurred or possibly even prevent installation.

Be cautious when making security permission changes. Your IT administrator needs to test to ensure that all of your firm's applications run without issue when reducing the security level of its user accounts from Administrator to Power User or User, before rolling out the changes to users.

Finally, you must have a proper backup solution designed to mitigate the effects of a ransomware infection. Ransomware has the capability to infect or run against any volume accessible from the infected computer, including any directly attached USB drives and even network drives. To combat this, we recommend that users disconnect USB drives directly attached to their computer systems or servers when not in use. Further, we recommend firms utilize an offsite backup solution in addition to having locally stored backups of your data. Backups, whether local or offsite, should always be encrypted. This way, if you were to become infected with a variant of ransomware, you would have the ability to restore the infected data from a recent backup. You want to make sure your solution provides that there is always a "clean" copy of your backup.

CHAPTER TWELVE

Case Management

If you still live in the paper world (and we still see lawyers who do!), you may not know that a case management application provides all of the functions that you are probably currently performing. You are most likely using some sort of system to organize your contacts. We don't see address books or a Rolodex any more. Lawyers collect contact information in an electronic form and synchronize it to mobile devices. You have a calendar to schedule events, which may be written in a day planner, but more likely, it is in electronic form as well. Deadlines and ticklers are put in the calendar as well. You have a file for each client or each client matter. These days, everyone seems to generate documents using a word processor and use email—darn near everyone has reached at least that point. You track everything you do for each client matter or keep some sort of diary. You probably even generate some sort of status concerning each matter. These are all functions of a case management system.

Even in a world full of smartphones and wireless devices, it amazes us that most solo and small firm lawyers still don't use a computerized case management software application. We've been making that statement for more than ten years now. Case management is a must-have for today's modern law office. You may have heard other terms that describe the same type of software. Vendors attempt to differentiate themselves by describing their products with different names. You may hear descriptions such as practice management, contact management, litigation management, matter management and so forth. Bottom line: They are all case management products, although they vary greatly in functionality. Arguably, the term practice management is more inclusive and encompasses what is termed "front office" (case/client information) and "back office" (accounting and billing).

There are several choices for case management, some of which we will cover here. The features vary by manufacturer, so make sure you understand what you're buying. Probably the feature we are asked about most is the integration of email and contacts with case management. Make sure that the product will work with your email system and that you understand how it may need to be configured. More and more of the case management choices synchronize with your electronic contact and calendar system (e.g. Outlook, Office 365, G Suite, etc.). Here are some questions to ask about synchronization support.

- How does the software deal with a common firm-wide Public Folder Calendar?
- Will the product synchronize with your iPad, smartphone or other mobile device?
- What if you don't have an Exchange server and use hosted Exchange services?
- What email clients are supported?
- Can you access your email using other devices and software, or are you restricted to using only the email interface of the case management software?
- Can you synchronize data with your Google account?
- Will synchronization occur wirelessly, or do you have to connect a cable and manually sync your data?
- Are IMAP (internet Message Access Protocol) connections supported or only POP3?
- Can you sync everything in your personal mailbox, or are you limited to a subset, such as contacts and calendar only and not the tasks?
- Will your data synchronize with Office 365?

There are two mistakes that we consistently see when firms decide to implement a case management system. The first mistake is the failure to require everyone in the firm to use the system. You will not realize the full return on your investment if only a few employees use it. In fact, it tends to cause a whole new set of problems, because sometimes there is crossover between lawyers and cases and some operate within the case management system and some don't. The second most common mistake is the failure to invest in training. Training will allow all employees to use the features of the case management system fully, thereby becoming more efficient and properly organizing all data for a client matter. Simply dumping a case management system into a firm is worse than useless. When you price the software, price the training as well.

As with other sections of this book, we cannot mention or address every case management package or every feature of every product. We mention the most popular and widely used case management packages that we see being used by solos and small firms.

In some of the software descriptions below, you will see that we are very critical of vendors who do not post pricing—they generally want to get you on the phone with someone from the sales department or give you an online demo, when all you want, in the beginning of your research, is some basic knowledge of features and pricing.

In the absence of pricing transparency by vendors, we encourage our readers to seek input from lawyers who actually use the products you are considering. Request specific references from vendors (though remember that those are likely to be cherry-picked!) and follow up on them. You will generally get some of the best counsel from practice management advisors. Listservs can be very helpful, as can local law practice management groups of state or local bar associations.

PracticeMaster

A highly rated case management application (and our personal favorite for an on-premise solution) is PracticeMaster (https://www.tabs3.com/products/practicemaster/practicemaster.html) by Software Technology, LLC, which is the choice of most solo and small firms in our area. Version 19.1 is the current shipping version of PracticeMaster. PracticeMaster comes in three versions: Multi-User, Platinum and Platinum SQL. The regular multi-user version of PracticeMaster contains a number of useful features that most lawyers would desire. Many solo and small firm lawyers think that Microsoft Outlook is a case management program. Not even close. You can view a chart that compares the features of Outlook and PracticeMaster at https://www.tabs3.com/products/practicemaster/comparison.html.

PracticeMaster and Tabs3 licenses include the first 12 months of maintenance. Perhaps it is a new trend to include maintenance automatically as a way to ensure that users pay for support. New in 2017 was the option to purchase PracticeMaster on a subscription plan. You still have the option of purchasing the software outright or get the same software and pay for it on a monthly basis, thereby avoiding the large upfront investment. The subscription pricing for PracticeMaster Platinum SQL is $32 per user per month. You can use the pricing estimator at https://www.tabs3.com/pricing-page/ to get immediate pricing up to five users. Just enter the number of concurrent users and the costs will be displayed for the multi-user version as well as what the monthly subscription cost will be. If you have six or more users, a custom price quote will be generated and sent to you.

Version 19.1 of PracticeMaster is the current shipping version and it includes several new features/enhancements. Some of the common highlights for PracticeMaster and Tabs3 include a new look with larger font, new color, theme, and navigation options. Quick Launch provides a search bar to search for actions, includes your recent matters and recent actions, and lets you pin and reorder frequently used matters and actions. There is also a new tabbed interface, which lets you quickly switch between windows. The user interface has a new home page, which provides a modern look and feel while keeping the accessibility of the classic Task Folders. Finally, each user can customize their own theme.

The PracticeMaster highlights include the following:

- Batch Journal Record Creation from Outlook—Added the ability to create journal records from multiple Outlook email messages at the same time.
- Designate Restricted Fields—Added the ability to prevent editing of specific fields by designating which users have rights to edit restricted fields in a file.
- Recap of Hours—New graphical Recap of Hours with daily, weekly, and monthly options that show billable and nonbillable hours and amounts and optionally include unprocessed timer records.
- Dashboard—New dashboard on the Home page shows the user's calendar, task list, and recap of hours.
- Outlook Plug-in—Added a new Attach PM Document button to the Outlook Plug-in toolbar that makes it easy to attach PracticeMaster documents while composing email in Outlook.

Mobile access requires the Platinum versions of PracticeMaster and Tabs3. With Tabs3 Connect, you have access to Tabs3 and PracticeMaster anywhere you can connect to the internet. This means you can get to your data from your smartphone or other mobile device. You have access to your client and contact information, fee and cost entry, personal and firm-wide calendar, and more. The connection is secured using SSL, and the data resides in your Tabs3/PracticeMaster environment in your office. The good news is that you can get Tabs3 Connect if you opt for the subscription pricing, which includes the Platinum SQL version. The monthly subscription pricing makes a lot of sense for solo and small firm attorneys, especially since you will get the best remote access solution to practice management data that we have ever seen (Tabs3 Connect).

Everything is moving to the cloud and PracticeMaster is too. You don't have to install PracticeMaster on your own local server. Software Technology, LLC has announced that ProCirrus (https://www.procirrus.com/) is its Preferred National Cloud Hosting Partner. ProCirrus is a full-service cloud hosting company that specializes in providing hosting services for the legal vertical and has extensive experience in hosting Tabs3 software.

Finally, it is highly recommended that you sign up for the free online demo of PracticeMaster. This will help you determine whether the product is right for your practice and your installed infrastructure. We don't think you can go wrong with this product. It is constantly being improved, and the support is among the best in the industry.

Clio

Clio (https://www.clio.com/) is a SaaS (software as a service) solution that is used by solo, small and midsized firms. Access is via an internet browser, which means it will work just fine on an Apple computer. The maker of Clio is Themis Solutions, Inc., which is headquartered in Vancouver, British Columbia. Themis Solutions has the excellent reputation for listening to its customers and constantly enhancing Clio based on users' suggestions. The company also has remote offices in Toronto, Calgary, and Dublin.

Clio is a full-featured practice management platform. Features such as document management and automation, time tracking, calendaring, tasks, billing, and so on provide a complete solution. The billing component works well for hourly, flat-fee, or contingency billing. In other words, Clio has been updated to provide more alternative billing options. Users have control over billing rates at the activity or matter level. Clio is highly customizable: custom fields can be inserted into any matter file. These custom fields have many different formats, so lawyers can enter dates, dollar amounts, website addresses, and various text types.

Clio integrates with many online service providers like Office 365, Box, Dropbox, Google Drive, Logikcull, NetDocuments, Fastcase, CloudMask, QuickBooks Online, and many others. You can see all the apps that integrate with Clio at https://www.clio.com/app-directory/. Like many other practice management products, Clio is constantly being improved, as can be seen by the increased integration with third-party products.

Clio Connect is a feature that enables firm members to share resources and collaborate with clients, contacts, or co-counsels easily through a secure web-based portal. This grants clients, contacts, or cocounsels the latitude to review and contribute to relevant matter developments and helps to mitigate associated inefficiencies related to time-consuming communications.

Clio provides extensive support to customers free of charge. Training webinars are available online, typically three days a week. Clio also offers a library of training articles and videos. Take advantage of the free trial to make sure Clio will work for you. The free trial period is only seven days, which really isn't enough time to play with all the features. We would suggest that you carve out some time each day to work with Clio during the trial period. You can also schedule a demo if that is more to your liking.

It is difficult to stay on top of all the news in the legal tech world and Clio added to that burden. As we were finalizing this book, Clio announced the acquisition of Lexicata at the annual Clio Cloud Conference in New Orleans. The acquisition of Lexicata, a legal client intake and client relationship management (CRM) solution, is a first step towards delivering a suite of products that's focused on creating a more client-centered approach to managing the end-to-end experience of working with a law firm. Instead of having to integrate with third-party providers, expect to see Clio becoming a multi-product service provider.

Clio is available in a tiered pricing model that adds additional features as you move up the tiers. The Starter level costs $39 per user per month (billed annually) and includes Case Management, Hourly and Flat Fee Billing, Custom Invoices, Time Tracking, Secure Client Portal: Clio Connect, Task Management, and Mobile Apps for iOS and Android Devices. The next level is the Boutique offering, which costs $59 per user per month (billed annually). It includes everything in the Starter version and adds Accounting Integrations, Integrated Credit Card Processor Clio Payments, Payment Plans, Custom Fields, Clio Launcher, Advanced Document Automation, Office 365 Business & Enterprise Integration, Trust Requests, Evergreen Retainers, Third Party Integration, and Alternative Fee Billing. The top tier is the Elite plan, which costs $99 per user per month (billed annually). It includes all the Boutique features plus Court Calendaring Rules, Matter Budgets, Campaign Tracker, Advanced Task Management, Advanced Reporting, Priority Support, and 1-on-1 Training.

There are no longer reduced costs for support staff. Clio considers a user to be a user. That means that a receptionist, paralegal, attorney, and so on will all pay the same price. Discounts are available as a member benefit from more than 35 state and municipal bar associations and the American Bar Association. Be sure to ask your bar association if a discount is available. The big news this year is that Clio eliminated legacy pricing for its long-term customers. This means that those loyal Clio customers that have been around for a long time will have to pay much more going forward. It will be interesting to see how much business Clio loses due to the price increase if previously loyal customers decide to abandon it. Make no mistake about it, Clio is a fine product and boasts the highest number of integrations to third-parties among the case management providers. However, it is also one of the most expensive of the cloud-based solutions.

Rocket Matter

Rocket Matter, around since 2007, is another web-based cloud practice management system designed specifically for the legal industry. It also contains a time and billing function, which provides almost all you need for your law practice. Rocket Matter has always been very popular among Macintosh users, as it is web-based. There really isn't any case management application that is specifically geared toward the Apple user community, so Rocket Matter meets that need through web browser access. You can still use Rocket Matter if you are a Windows shop, since all you need is an internet connection and a web browser.

Rocket Matter has continued to evolve over the years and like most cloud-based case management systems, releases improvements and enhancements in an ongoing fashion. Rocket Matter even has an app specifically designed for iOS and Android devices.

A recent enhancement is Rocket Matter Project Management. Project Management is a new workflow management platform for law firms. The Project Management feature enables attorneys to easily create transitions between different phases of a case. Each phase can contain its own calendar calculations, custom data, and tasks, allowing legal professionals to set up automated systems so that they never miss deadlines. When a matter is switched from one phase to another, all of this predefined data automatically appears in Rocket Matter. Besides workflows, users have access to sophisticated reporting tools to reveal the status of matters through the various phases. For example, you can easily tell how many matters are in each phase, which are on schedule, and which are overdue. Since Project Management also integrates with Communicator, you can get alerts on your mobile devices when the status of a matter changes.

In 2017, to celebrate its 10th anniversary, Rocket Matter released a new version called Atlas Gold Edition. According to the press release, Atlas Gold has a redesigned mobile application, powerful collaboration tools and more ways to boost profits and increase efficiency. Rocket Matter now has a secure messaging tool called Communicator. Communicator functions similarly to tools such as HipChat or Slack and is built into the core Rocket Matter application. You can even set calendar appointments and transfer files with Communicator.

Not to be outdone, Rocket Matter released a new version of the cloud offering called Braavos in early October 2018. Braavos is the first of a series of dramatic new application improvements and practice area-specific add-on modules. As an example, Braavos includes a new optional add-on module for Insurance Defense firms, which greatly simplifies the arduous tasks these law firms face when billing their clients.

Some other new features are bulk payments and adjustments for invoices as well as an Insurance Defense Package for LEDES (Legal Electronic Data

Exchange Standard) billing. You can now take a single payment and apply it to multiple invoices. Rocket Matter's Insurance Defense module helps solve common e-billing headaches that defense firms deal with by providing the following features:

- Customize your LEDES headers
- Leverage intelligent invoice analysis
- Update LEDES invoice with bulk actions
- Pair LEDES files with invoices
- Automate adjustments
- Track collection with insurance defense reporting

Rocket Matter integrates with a lot of third party services such as Dropbox, Office 365, QuickBooks Online, Ruby Receptionist, etc. Check the website to see if your favorite third party tools is supported by Rocket Matter.

We are happy to say that Rocket Matter, as opposed to many others, is transparent with its pricing and has it posted on the website. The cost is $55 per user per month when billed annually. It is $65 per user per month on a month-to-month basis. There is no tiered pricing as with Clio. Each user is charged $55 and gets all of the features and integrations along with unlimited support too. There is a free seven-day trial available, but that's not much time to run the software through its paces. We would recommend starting with the trial. If it appears as if Rocket Matter will meet your needs, go with the month-to-month option ($65/user/month) initially and then go with the $55 cost if you feel you want to stick with the product.

Rocket Matter is a cloud implementation and carries the same issues as other providers. The data is held by a third party even though it is transmitted on an encrypted channel. Those who have used Rocket Matter generally give it favorable reviews, and we recommend that solos and small firms that want a cloud solution take a look at Rocket Matter and MyCase. Both are fine products.

MyCase

We are seeing a great deal of interest in another web-based case management product. MyCase is similar to the other products and provides similar functions, such as shared firm calendars and reminders, tasks, contact management, document organization, document assembly, time and billing, and so on. MyCase differentiates itself from other cloud-based case management offerings by providing a MyCase website. Actually, the value of the website is working as a portal for clients to get information about their case, pay their invoices, and securely communicate with the firm. Besides the portal aspects, MyCase can provision a website that integrates with the MyCase application (that's where the client portal feature comes in) and includes:

- Modern legal website with a mobile responsive design
- Custom logo design
- Domain purchasing and website hosting
- Professional content writing and HD images
- Essential Search Engine Optimization (SEO)
- Google Analytics account to track your site's success
- Blogging, social media & professional association links
- MyCase Client Portal and Online Payments integration
- Ongoing support for content updates and additions

The website feature costs a onetime setup fee of $995 and then $50 a month.

MyCase prides itself in providing enhancements that the customers want. Even though you would use a browser to access MyCase from your computer, you have the option of using a native iOS or Android app from your mobile device. The MyCase app gives you access to all of your case information and billing history while on the road. You even have the ability to send secure email messages from the app, bill and track time, and get real-time notifications about important meetings, document uploads and more.

MyCase is constantly being updated, sometimes as often as a few times a week. Users get a notification of new/updated features via a What's New Bubble on the screen. Updates are also identified in the customer newsletter. Some of the recent updates fall into three major areas, collaboration, efficiencies, and getting paid. Some of the collaboration features include access to staff calendars in the app, access to firm and case documents, and direct messaging. Efficiency for your firm is achieved through features such as batch document uploads and downloads, automatic saving of notes, defining default folder structures, calendaring, etc. Another efficiency item is integration with Dropbox, where a Dropbox folder is created in MyCase. You can work natively in Dropbox and the updates are instantly reflected in MyCase. Reporting helps run your firm in an efficient manner as well. There are now 16 built-in reports with the Case Revenue Report and Fee Allocation Report being the newest. Finally, getting paid is certainly a very important aspect of your practice. MyCase helps by having multiple timers, time tracking on mobile devices, LEDES formatted invoices, automated invoice reminders to clients, link for payments without requiring usage of the portal, etc.

MyCase costs $39 per user per month when billed annually. It will cost you $49 per user per month if you opt for month-to-month payments. There is a free 30-day trial, which we recommend you take advantage of. MyCase is one of the lower cost cloud-based case management offerings. Don't think that you get less function because of the lower cost. Not so. MyCase is gaining in popularity and interest, primarily due to the features to cost ratio. Given Clio's pricing, we suggest that you look to MyCase and Rocket Matter first.

CosmoLex

Another cloud-based case management product that is getting a lot of buzz on the message boards is CosmoLex. Unlike the other cloud-based offerings, CosmoLex started out as a billing package and moved into case management. The others started as contact/matter managers and added billing.

CosmoLex has all the basics that a solo or small firm lawyer is looking for in a case management system. Included features are calendar & task, email management, custom fields, document assembly, document management, practice dashboard, and secure client portal. From the billing side there is time & expense tracking, billing & payments, and electronic (LEDES) billing. Trust accounting and accounts payable functions are included as well. A real differentiator for CosmoLex is the lack of QuickBooks integration. QuickBooks is not needed because all of QuickBook's functions are included within the CosmoLex product.

Another benefit to CosmoLex is its partnership with LawPay. The CosmoLex partnership means that there is no fixed monthly fee for using LawPay to handle credit card transactions. Other case management platforms also work with LawPay, but there will be a fixed monthly fee in addition to the normal per transaction processing fees.

Another change as we were finalizing this book is the announcement that CosmoLex has been acquired by Software Technology, LLC. That positions CosmoLex as the cloud offering in the Tabs3/Practice Master family. If you want an on-premise solution for practice management and billing, go to the Tab3 and PracticeMaster offerings. Cloud-based practice management and billing would land with the CosmoLex offering. Finally, if you just want cloud billing then Kurent is your choice. It looks like CosmoLex is a great choice for those long time Tabs3/PracticeMaster users that want to migrate to the cloud.

The cost of CosmoLex is $59 per user per month when billed on an annual basis. The cost would be $69 per user if you don't want to be billed annually and choose the month-to-month option instead. When you subscribe to CosmoLex, your external accountant or bookkeeper gets free access as an added benefit. Like the other offerings, there is a free trial period to help with your decision process. We recommend you take advantage of the trial, which is 14 days instead of the seven days offered by some others.

Time Matters

LexisNexis has a couple of offerings suitable for the solo and small firm market. Time Matters (https://www.lexisnexis.com/business-of-law/products/practice-management/time-matters) used to be one of the most popular case management package for solo and small firms (before being purchased by LexisNexis), but we don't see it at very many firms in our area. Time Matters is a very powerful and highly customizable case management application, but it can also be fairly complicated for many small firm lawyers. It is an absolute necessity to purchase training if you are considering implementing Time Matters in your firm. We won't spend a lot of time going over Time Matters as we don't feel that it is appropriate to pursue, especially with so many cloud-based products being used by solo and small firm attorneys.

Others

Additional products are available, but some of the vendors aren't public with the cost or system requirements. We are less than impressed with companies that aren't open about their pricing and technical requirements. Products like ProLaw (Thomson Elite) require you to fill out a contact form so that a representative can contact you about pricing. We are not fond of this practice and recommend a relationship with more open vendors, especially when you are entering this arena and want to make an apples-to-apples comparison. The good news is there are a lot more options for case management products as time moves on. The majority of the newcomers to the case management arena are cloud-based instead of on-premise solutions. It seems like we hear of several new cloud-based solutions every year. The move to the cloud has been fairly dramatic over the past couple of years!

CHAPTER THIRTEEN

Time and Billing Software

Probably the second most important function of your law practice is billing your clients for services rendered. Practicing law is clearly the most important, but getting paid is second, thereby ensuring the continued success and sustainability of your practice. Lawyers tend to hate the billing process and are not much fonder of the software that helps them generate invoices. Some solos and small firms still generate invoices manually, although their numbers are diminishing. We'll look at several options and try to give you some guidance.

You have a lot of options for generating your bills, from a completely manual system to the fully automatic capture and assembly of invoices. Two components make up the items in your bills. One is time. This component is calculated by taking the hourly rate and applying it to the amount of time spent on a task. You can capture this time manually or automatically while the task is being accomplished. Flat fees are also considered time components, where the dollar amount is applied irrespective of the time spent. The second component is the fixed-cost items of the invoice. This would include such expenses as postage, copier costs, filing fees, courier charges, and any other fixed fees. As with the time components, you can track these expenses manually or automatically (to some level or another) through the use of technology.

We are seeing more and more firms adopting some sort of alternative fee arrangements (AFAs) for their practice. It may be flat fee only or a hybrid type of billing with a flat-fee portion and an hourly portion. AFAs are more complicated to automate because of the various customized rules that may apply. The good news is that many of the software packages are sophisticated enough to handle customized rules and they are getting better and better as time goes by. You may have to deal with some manual override techniques if the billing software can't accommodate a particular AFA scenario that you want to implement.

As in other sections of this book, we'll try to cover a lot of the billing methods and applications that we see being used by the solo and small firm attorneys. This will not be an all-inclusive list, so if your favorite product isn't mentioned, it probably means that we've never seen it being used by solo or small firms.

Manual Generation

Pencil and paper are the simplest way to capture time and expense. With manual generation, however, you must remember to log your time and the number of copies or whatever other chargeable component needs to be tracked. Make no mistake about it, studies have shown over and over again that this manual tracking results in a lot of lost time and expense. Because a lawyer's time equals money, many lawyers are shortchanging themselves by not moving to a technology-based solution. Some studies place these uncaptured costs at the 20 percent to 30 percent range and sometimes higher.

Nevertheless, if this is what you do, on a periodic basis (daily, monthly, the end of the case, and so forth), you total the charges and generate the bill. Many solo practitioners start by using a word processing package to generate their bills to save some money. These bills are professional enough in appearance but still require manually adding up numbers and multiplying other numbers. Moreover, another method is needed to keep track of payments made by the client and/or transfers of funds from other sources, such as a trust account. As the practice becomes more complicated, the billing process becomes more susceptible to mistakes.

If you must start with a manual method for generating your invoices, invest in billing software as soon as possible to improve your accuracy, maximize your income, and minimize your losses.

Accounting Software—QuickBooks

Some lawyers are actually using a financial accounting package to generate their bills. Certainly the most popular software application we see is QuickBooks by Intuit (https://quickbooks.intuit.com/). Using QuickBooks to generate invoices allows the firm to have a total financial package, where all sorts of financial reports are available. However, productivity reports are not available. You won't be able to determine easily how many billable hours are attributed to a specific individual or how much money you lost due to write-offs.

The 2018 ABA Legal Technology Survey stated that solo and small firm attorneys are asked "write-off" billed expense 5 percent to 9 percent of the time, so this may be more important than you might have thought! One advantage of QuickBooks is the ability to generate payroll. This may not be a compelling reason for many lawyers, especially given the added cost, complexity, and reporting requirements. In general, it is more cost effective to use a third-party service provider such as ADP or Paychex to handle solo and small firm payrolls. QuickBooks can also handle processing of credit card payments, thereby integrating another piece of the financials into a single product. We hear that most lawyers began using QuickBooks because their accountant told them to. This sure makes it simpler for the accountant! Make sure your accountant sets up your chart of accounts in QuickBooks so you know where certain charges and fees should go. Your CPA should be familiar with financials for a law firm. If not, it's probably time to look for a new accountant.

QuickBooks comes in several different versions—even an online version that allows access from any computer and does not require installation of any software. We don't recommend using the online version, as it requires that your data be stored at Intuit. Your financial data is highly sensitive, and we recommend that you control your own data and not risk compromise by holding it at a third-party site. Consider, too, the possibly severe consequences if the third party is "down" and you can't manage the financial part of your law practice. Generally, cloud service providers are fairly reliable, but there are no guarantees when dealing with technology.

Since QuickBooks is an accounting package, some knowledge of financial principles is helpful. You will need to set up a chart of accounts for your practice. We recommend consulting with your accountant before configuring QuickBooks so that your financial categories are consistent with the accountant's needs and your business needs. If you are new to QuickBooks, consider purchasing a support plan to help you learn the features of the software and get technical help. Many local community colleges also offer evening classes for QuickBooks, which would be a relatively inexpensive way to get some training in how to use the product.

The desktop versions of QuickBooks vary in cost based on the capabilities of the software and number of concurrent licenses that are needed. The Pro version costs $299.95 (prior to any discounts) for a single user, and the Premier version cost $499.95 (prior to any discounts) for a single user. The Enterprise version is sold only on a subscription basis with varying subscription levels. You can elect to run the Enterprise version on your own server or purchase Enterprise with hosting. The Enterprise version is intended for larger organizations and can scale to a million names (e.g. customers, vendors, employees) and up to 30 users.

Most solo and small firms will find that QuickBooks Pro is more than sufficient for their needs. In previous years, Intuit offered a three-pack license at a reduced rate over the single-user cost directly from its website. The three-pack is no longer a separate product, and you'll need to order three separate licenses if you need that many users. The good news is that the traditional multiuser discount is applied. The single-user price is $299.95. Selecting two users will cost $549.95, or $274.98 per user. Three users will cost $799.95, or $266.65 per user.

To enhance its desktop offering, Intuit has QuickBooks Pro Plus 2018, which is an annual subscription product that includes unlimited support, automatic online data backup, and upgrades. The cost is $299.95 per user per year. Phone support is available on a 24/7 basis. You also receive upgrades as they are released. That would save you from spending money to upgrade with each edition (yearly). The $299.99 per-year cost seems rather high to us, especially since you'll be spending money year after year. We recommend purchasing the standard QuickBooks Pro software and upgrading the version every three years. That will save you several hundred dollars over the life of the software.

The QuickBooks Premier version contains additional features for specific industries and expanded reporting capabilities. As an example, you can track unbilled time and expenses for professional services; set different billing rates by employee, client, and service; and analyze profitability by matter. QuickBooks Premier 2018 is $499.95 (prior to any discounts) per user. Like QuickBooks Pro, there is a QuickBooks Premier Plus 2018 version that includes support, backup, and updates. The cost of QuickBooks Premier Plus 2018 is the same, $499.95 (prior to any discounts) per user per year.

It appears that Intuit will no longer offer upgrade pricing. In the past, if you owned an older version of QuickBooks, you could get a reduced price for upgrading to the newer version. Not anymore. There is no incentive for being a loyal QuickBooks user. You have to pay the same price as a new user would. Intuit, like many other application providers, is trying to migrate users to a subscription cloud service. That way it gets a constant revenue stream. Microsoft is doing the same thing with Office 365. At some point, and we're getting closer every year, vendors will no longer offer local loaded applications and everything will be in the cloud. To that end, there are now five versions of QuickBooks Online—Self-Employed, Simple Start, Essentials, Plus, and Advanced. Each edition adds additional features to the previous edition. As an example, Essentials adds manage bills, multiple users and track time to the Simple Start features. The monthly cost (prior to any discounts) for the QuickBooks Online versions are $10 for Self-Employed, $20 for Simple Start, $35 for Essentials, $60 for Plus, and $150 for Advanced.

Mac users no longer have the option to run QuickBooks locally and must choose one of the online cloudbased versions.

Accountants love it when lawyers use QuickBooks as their billing software. They can take the QuickBooks data file at the end of the year and generate tax returns with relative ease. However, we don't recommend using QuickBooks for billing for several reasons. First, the invoices are very sterile looking and have very little room for customization. The data is there and clients can understand the information, but the invoice format lacks any capability for graphics, different fonts, custom text to identify different sections, or rearrangement of how the information appears on the page. Showing remaining balances properly is an issue too—a real problem if you want to show trust account balances and transfers or automatically indicate how much of the evergreen retainer needs to be replenished. As previously mentioned, QuickBooks Pro won't provide you with any productivity reports unless you purchase the Premier version. You're going to have to find a different way to determine how many write-down hours an associate had for a month or the amount of no-charge entries by client. In spite of these limitations, we still see a lot of lawyers using QuickBooks.

Billing Specific

There are a few products that specifically address the billing needs of lawyers. Attorneys have some special requirements for handling the billing financials such as trust accounts, retainers, etc. We are seeing more and more attorneys using the billing function contained within their cloud-based practice management platform (e.g. Clio, MyCase, Rocket Matter, etc.), but there are still some billing specific options for the solo and small firm lawyer.

Timeslips

Arguably the most popular billing software among solo and small firm lawyers is Timeslips by Sage (https://www.sage.com/en-us/products/sage-timeslips/). Timeslips is a billing-specific software package that generates bills, tracks receivables, and manages trust accounting. We see many Timeslips installations in solo and small firm offices, especially those that have no case management system. Even so, we are beginning to see firms implementing invoicing products that are included with the integrated solutions that we describe later in this chapter.

Probably one of the reasons for the popularity of Timeslips is that it can be configured specifically for the legal industry right out of the box and supports the LEDES (Legal Electronic Data Exchange Standard) billing format with the optional electronic billing module. When you first install Timeslips, you select the type of business. This configures Timeslips to use the types of tasks and expenses that are specific to the industry.

As an example, when you select the legal profession, default tasks are automatically created that deal with those items that are performed in the law office. There will be tasks for consultations, document review, depositions, and so forth. The expense names are also automatically created and include such costs as copier usage, courier fees, postage, filing fees, and the like. Trust accounting is also built into Timeslips, which is another reason the software is very popular in solo and small firm offices. You can configure Timeslips to deduct fees earned from the trust account automatically or leave it as a manual transfer process. In addition, Timeslips can automatically create the dollar amount to place on the invoice to bring the retainer amount back to a set level. This is a very popular feature for those attorneys who have evergreen retainer arrangements.

Timeslips is licensed on a per-machine basis. Each computer that needs to access Timeslips will require the purchase of a license. In a small office, it is often the case that only one computer is used to process billing. The timekeepers (typically lawyers) may elect to track their time manually on paper and give the time sheets to the office manager or bookkeeper for entry into Timeslips. This arrangement keeps licensing costs down and allows for growth in the law firm. As the firm grows, additional licenses may be purchased and network access configured for the Timeslips database. You can use Timeslips in a Microsoft terminal server environment as well. Each person that uses a terminal server connection will need a license as each connection is handled just like a physical computer.

The current version is Sage Timeslips 2019 and it is compatible with Windows 10. Last year, Sage threatened to cease selling Timeslips as a purchased product and force users to purchase an annual subscription. In other words Timeslips 2018 was supposed to be the last version that you could purchase outright. We're sure that produced a lot of revenue for Sage as people scrambled to get the last version and avoid getting locked into an annual subscription cost model. Apparently, there was a HUGE pushback from the current installed client base. The good news is that you still have the option to purchase the product outright or go with an annual subscription.

Sage has completely changed the way you access information about Timeslips. In the past, you could see a complete feature list, support options and even purchase the software online. Not anymore. You have to contact Sage if you want to find out what the cost will be, what support packages are available or just general information. Sage always offers discounts in the August/September time period for the new version so that would be the best time to buy if you are interested. Expect to pay several hundreds of dollars per user for the purchased version. Our experience has been that the cost per user almost doubles if you add a maintenance plan. Frankly, we would not recommend purchasing maintenance. The cost is way too high and the product is very stable now so you shouldn't have to contact support. Put your money towards a good Timeslips consultant if you have questions or need to know how to accomplish something in Timeslips. Our recommendation is to purchase the product and consider upgrades every three years. Sage only supports the three latest versions so it makes sense to always be using a supported product.

Kurent

New to the scene in 2017 was a cloud-based billing package by Tabs3. The first released version was pretty basic and only handled the simplest of billing needs. Kurent has evolved and allows you to bill your clients using hourly, contingency, flat fee, and electronic task-based billing such as LEDES. There are flexible invoicing options and layouts available. You can add your firm's logo and deliver invoices via email, printed copy or downloaded PDF.

Kurent presents the user with a master dashboard, which makes it easy to track matter information. Every screen has four Quick Launch icons that make it easy to perform basic billing tasks. In less than two minutes, you can add a fee, a cost item, create a matter or generate an invoice. In addition, trust accounting is now available with Kurent. Kurent's Contacts and Matters will sync with QuickBooks' Customers and Jobs. A change made in Kurent will automatically be made in QuickBooks and vice versa. You can also sync receipts to QuickBooks income accounts. Clients can pay you online with credit cards or E-Checks through a client portal powered by LawPay.

Kurent costs $26 per user per month when billed annually. The cost is only $29 per user per month if you don't want to commit to an annual payment. There is a 30-day trial available, which we highly recommend you take advantage of.

Billing Software for Macs

There are not that many legal-specific billing software applications for Mac computers. Most Mac users will migrate toward web-based products for their firms. There are some native Mac applications, but like the Windows world, more and more users are moving toward the cloud.

EasyTime

Many of the practice management implementations also include some sort of billing mechanism, so you may not need a separate software application. We'll mention a few of the billing packages that are available for the Mac, but we certainly can't mention them all. One such stand-alone package for the Mac is EasyTime. EasyTime, by Bright Light Software (http://brightlight software.com/), runs natively on Mac OS X and does not require any third-party database packages. The current shipping version is 4.0.18, released November 22, 2017. It requires Mac OS 10.10 or higher. The cost is $199 for a single user and $50 if you are upgrading from version 3. If you need a network version, you'll have to use version 3 as there is no network version available for version 4. The cost of EasyTime 3—Network Version is $249.

There is a 30 day trial available for EasyTime so you can try it before you buy it. It is fully functional during the trial period. Once you purchase EasyTime, you will receive a license code via email to activate the product and continue usage beyond the trial period. As you can see from the pricing, EasyTime is a very affordable billing package for the solo and small firm attorney that runs natively on macOS.

Billings Pro

Another popular package is Billings Pro (https://www.marketcircle.com/billingspro/) by Marketcircle. The Billings Pro cost model is based on how many invoices, statements, or estimates you generate per month. The Freelance plan costs $5 per user per month and limits you to five invoices, five estimates, and five statements per month. This plan doesn't seem to be very practical unless you only have a couple of very large clients and don't invoice all that often. The Professional plan is $10 per user per month for unlimited invoices, estimates, and statements per month. Since there is no contract commitment with Billings Pro, we recommend starting with the Professional plan. If it looks like Billings Pro is something that works for your firm, then convert to the Professional Yearly plan, which costs $99 for a full year. Additional users are also $99 per user for the year.

A big concern with the Billings Pro cloud offering is that its data center is located in another country. Your data is stored locally and gets synchronized to servers in Canada, meaning that you can continue to work if the network is unavailable or the servers are unreachable. Some attorneys may feel that storing billing information for their clients in another country is not a problem and accept potential cross-border issues. Of course, Canadian attorneys welcome the fact that the servers are in their own country.

As with most of the products mentioned, be sure to take advantage of the free 30-day trial before purchase.

Integrated Packages

Many of the case management products support integration with billing packages. This means that you enter your information into the case management system and the time or expense is automatically captured for the billing process. There are advantages to using the same vendor for your case management and billing needs. The products are designed to work together and share information in a very efficient manner. However, selecting these all-in-one packages may not give you the best features of each package. If you really want a "best of breed" implementation, then make sure you investigate how the case management and billing packages share the data. Many case management applications provide links to billing packages by other vendors. Be careful to understand how to configure these links, especially if it is a manual process. We've seen clients who added tasks to their case management software and forgot to define the linkage to their billing software. This means that you may not bill for the effort when you use these newly defined tasks. Given the potential for error when trying to build your own solution, our recommendation is to use the billing function(s) for the vendor that provides your case management platform.

PCLaw

LexisNexis has a couple of billing options to address the needs of solo and small firm law offices. A very popular package is PCLaw. The current version is PCLaw 16.3 (https://www.lexisnexis.com/business-of-law/products/practice-management/pclaw#). PCLaw includes some features that you would expect from a case management system. You can keep track of contacts, calendar entries, phone calls, notes, tasks, and so on. This choice may be a good alternative for a solo practitioner to keep start-up costs down since it includes basic case management functions along with billing in a single package.

The full feature set of PCLaw is no longer available on the website. Like other LexisNexis products, you have to complete a form to see a demo or get further product information. Lexis has provided a web page (https://help-blss.lexisnexis.com/PCLaw/16/Content/2-WHATS-NEW.htm) that lists the new features for each release of version 16. Some of the features include Charts (Visual Analytics), View Productivity Reports in Excel, Simplified Template Editor with Element Sizing and Positioning Tool, View Last Receipt Date in Matter Manager, Client Work-In-Progress Report and Changing G/L accounts on Paid Payable Entries (Accrual Systems).

The pricing is no longer available on the LexisNexis website for the public to view. LexisNexis advertises that you can get PCLaw for as low as $39 per user per month. When you click the "Buy Now" button you are sent to a page to fill out a form to contact an expert. As we've mentioned before, this is not a practice that we are fond of, and we recommend using products from vendors that are transparent with their pricing. There is a footnote about the $39 price. It is based on five users over a three year period and includes maintenance. That means your out-of-pocket cost for PCLaw will run at least $7,020 for the three year period.

Juris is another billing software application offered by LexisNexis. It is typically used by larger law firms or in integrating with Time Matters. We have never seen Juris used in a solo or small firm setting. As with some of the other products mentioned, you have to contact Lexis to get pricing information.

Tabs3

Another popular billing package is Tabs3 by Software Technology, LLC. Tabs3 is the companion product to PracticeMaster, which is Software Technology's case management software. Tabs3 pricing is based on the number of billable entities. Like so many other vendors, the cost of the software includes the first year of maintenance. The single-user version of Tab3 is $445 for one timekeeper and increases to $695 for five timekeepers. You'll need to purchase the multi-user version if you need more than one person accessing the data at the same time.

You can use the pricing calculator (https://www.tabs3.com/pricing-page/) on the website to determine the cost for five or fewer users. Fill out the form if you have six or more users to get a custom quote.

You can now purchase Tabs3 on a subscription basis, which may be a good cost effective alternative to outright software purchase for the solo and small firm lawyer. The best part is that you get Tabs3 Connect included with all subscription purchases, which is a killer remote access solution. The cost is a very affordable $32 per month per timekeeper. Adding General Ledger, Accounts Payable and Trust Account is only an additional $8 per month per timekeeper for all three financial options.

Version 19.1 of Tabs3 is the current shipping version. Refer to the PracticeMaster section in the case management chapter to see the common new items for both PracticeMaster and Tabs3 in version 19.

The Tabs3 highlights for version 19 include:

- **Tabs3 Online Payments**—Added the ability to include a ProPay payment link with your emailed statements allowing clients to pay their bill online.
- **Recap of Hours**—New graphical Recap of Hours with daily, weekly, and monthly options that shows billable and non-billable hours and amounts.
- **Reorder Fees on Statements**—The new Reorder Fees utility allows you to change the order in which fees with the same date appear on statements.
- **Write-Up/Write-Down Fees and Costs Across Matters**—You can now write-up or write-down all matters for a client at the same time.
- **Apply Payments to Multiple Matters**—Payments for multiple matters can now be applied to individual statements.
- **Better Handling of Credit Transactions**—Entering credits for paid transactions will automatically apply the credit to accounts receivable when the statement is updated. Produce a credit memo by running a statement with only credit transactions.

Unlike other billing packages, Tabs3 has separated out various financial functions and priced them as individual components. As an example, there are additional components such as trust accounting, general ledger, and accounts payable. This means that you can expand Tabs3 from a pure billing package into a complete accounting package. You can find more information about Tabs3 at https://www.tabs3.com/. We regard Tabs3 as highly as we do its case management counterpart, PracticeMaster. It also consistently receives high ratings from legal software experts.

Final Thoughts

One of the higher-level (expensive) billing alternatives is provided by ProLaw, which is a Thomson Reuters Elite product. ProLaw is an integrated package, and the billing component is not available as a separate function. Very few solos and small law firms have chosen this route in our experience.

Most of our clients who use stand-alone applications have chosen QuickBooks or Timeslips for billing, and they are generally quite happy with what they have chosen—although everything has a learning curve. All of these vendors are happy to let you sample their product in one manner or another, so don't hesitate to try before you buy. Also, if you aren't keen on accounting, talk to your friends who are equally numbers-challenged and see what has worked for them. In many cases, the choice has been made by someone at the firm who is going to perform the accounting or bookkeeping functions, and that's fine. As long as you stay with one of the "majors," you won't be left scrambling to find someone who knows your obscure time and billing package if that person leaves.

CHAPTER FOURTEEN

Document Management

Document management software solutions can be relatively expensive for the solo or small firm operation, although there are some cost-effective alternatives. Several of the better-known document management products tend to be used more for enterprise-size companies because of their cost and complexity. As the industry matures, vendors are merging the functions of document management, content management, and knowledge management. This is especially true as electronic files have become a critical component of discovery. You may see applications described as document management systems, content management systems, knowledge management systems, or even enterprise content management systems. Just because a vendor chooses to describe its product using particular words doesn't mean there is anything unique or special about it. In general, all of the terms previously mentioned are used for applications that organize information.

The main purpose of a document management system is to organize information into a usable and searchable form. How many times have you looked for a file or document but couldn't remember the name or location? A document management system allows for fast and easy access to the data, whether in paper or electronic form. It also provides access control and enforceability of rules. As an example, perhaps one of your rules is that every document has a specific category (programmed ahead of time) tagged to it. This makes for consistency and removes the human error in typing or misspelling the category tag. In addition, security is another feature of document management systems. Typically, you can set security access to particular matters, specific types of files, or even unique files themselves. One person could have full control over a document, whereas another might be able to view the content but not modify it.

According to the 2018 ABA Legal Technology Survey Report, the top document management software offerings used by attorneys are iManage (27 percent), Worldox (14 percent), NetDocuments (13 percent), and Time Matters

(11 percent). Time Matters is really a practice management platform with capabilities to manage documents. Many of the practice management products (e.g. PracticeMaster, Clio, etc.) have document management features.

iManage

It is really hard to stay current with a product that changes names and companies so many times over its life. Several years ago, we knew it as Interwoven. Then it was known as Autonomy iManage WorkSite. Autonomy then became an HP company, and the product name changed to just WorkSite. A management buyout of the business from HP in July of 2015 leaves us with the current name of iManage Work. There is a cloud solution in addition to on premise software. iManage Work now includes Artificial Intelligence (AI) ready functionality and fully integrates with Microsoft Office, including Office 365.

You will need to contact iManage in order to get costs and request a demo. Expect to pay thousands of dollars for this system. It is a highly regarded document management environment (if you can remember the name) but is also geared more toward the intermediate to large-scale firms.

Worldox

The most popular and most used document management system for solo and small firm operations is Worldox (https://www.worldox.com/). We can confirm that since a large portion of our client base is solo and small firm attorneys. Worldox is licensed on a concurrent-user basis and not per seat. The current shipping version of Worldox is GX4. GX4 Professional is the standard network client server installation that has been around for ages. It is the traditional desktop version.

The next version is Worldox Enterprise, which is adapted for multi-office, remote access environments. It is typically hosted at a data center and has full communication with local applications, including Microsoft Office, Outlook, and third-party products such as case management. The final version of Worldox is a SaaS hosted solution called Worldox Cloud. With the Worldox Cloud solution, your data is hosted on Worldox servers in its data centers. GX4 utilizes Active Profiling technology for ease of use and automation, enabling you to manage, share, and access all your digital content effortlessly. Worldox GX4 also facilitates effortless content sharing with connectors to industry standard applications like Citrix ShareFile and Legal Anywhere.

The pricing for Worldox is no longer available on the website. You have to fill out a form online in order to request one of the following items.

- Schedule an information call
- Have a Worldox representative contact you
- Schedule an online demo
- Request an evaluation copy
- Place an order

Worldox GX4 Professional is licensed on a per concurrent user basis, which makes it very affordable for solo and small firms, especially since there are no minimum seat purchase requirements. New orders do require you to purchase mandatory annual maintenance. No separate server is required and the indexer service can be run on any workstation-class computer. The computer resource requirements for Worldox are very light when compared to other document management systems. The application is very robust and easy to use, hence its popularity within the legal community.

Worldox Enterprise is intended for multiple offices and remote access environments. It looks and acts just like the local desktop (GX4 Professional) version. Worldox also offers a Worldox Web, which extends the power of Worldox so that users can access their documents from anywhere, anytime, from virtually any devices. Worldox Web works seamlessly and adapts invisibly to:

- Web-browser equipped notebooks and desktops
- iOS Devices
- Android Devices
- BlackBerry Devices

A key point to remember about true document management applications is their stringent enforcement of the classification rules. The user must use the system within the configured rules, which sometimes frustrates people because of the rigid requirements. In contrast, applications that are not specifically document management software aren't restrictive or mandatory. The danger is that data may be lost or misfiled when the rules are not stringently enforced. Worldox is an excellent choice for document management, as it integrates with almost every case management system available. It consistently receives good reviews from legal software experts.

NetDocuments

NetDocuments is a popular SaaS provider for document management. Many law firms, small to large, have had great experiences with NetDocuments.

We have heard lawyers say that it was very easy to install and configure. In one case, a lawyer converted his firm (tens of thousands of documents) over to NetDocuments in a weekend all by himself.

NetDocuments provides all of the features you would expect in a document management system, in addition to matter-centric work spaces, email management, collaboration, mobile access and governance. NetDocuments has always been cloud-based and provides a very secure environment. You can monitor user activity, which effectively provides you with a data loss prevention (DLP) system in addition to a document management platform. NetDocuments has cloaked its pricing, which seems to be a trending practice among legal technology providers. You can no longer determine the costs without filling out a form to request a demo and waiting for someone to contact you. So much for transparency.

NetDocuments is highly regarded in the legal marketplace. In our experience, we see NetDocuments primarily used in larger firms, whereas Worldox is present in more solo and small firm environments.

Plain Folders

Finally, a very simple form of document management for solo and small firms (though not what we would recommend) is to follow a standard folder and file naming convention along with search software. Other than the potential cost for search software, this is a very low-cost solution. Some lawyers will use the search capabilities of Windows or Mac before even investing in supplemental search software. Typically, folders are named on a client or client-matter basis. Files are then given a very descriptive name, such as <client name> followed by the file purpose and sometimes the date. As an example, "Franklin request for admissions.doc" would be the filename for your request for admissions in the Franklin matter. This is a very manageable method to organize data when your practice is small. As your practice grows, search software may be needed to assist in finding particular files pertaining to specific issues.

Final Thoughts

If you are considering the purchase of a document management system, Worldox is an excellent first choice. We have implemented this software many times, and clients are always happy with it. We have become big fans over many years. No matter what product you are considering, see whether there is a trial version available, or at least participate in a demo of the product, to determine if it meets your firm's needs.

CHAPTER FIFTEEN

Document Assembly

Essentially, document assembly software automates the creation of legal documents that are used repeatedly. This includes such documents as wills, leases, contracts and letters. You can think of document assembly as templates that can be used over and over. This shortens the time for document preparation and increases the efficiency of your practice. If you use flat fees, document assembly can be a godsend for filling the law firm coffers in less time.

Document assembly software can be specialized for a particular industry or can be generic. As an example, specialized document assembly software is typically used in estate planning and tax preparation. In those situations, the user answers questions in a survey type of form and then the required documents are generated using the answers provided. If you have ever used one of the personal income tax programs (e.g., TurboTax, H&R Block, etc.), you've seen how document assembly works. You may see the term "document automation," but it means the same thing as document assembly for our discussion.

HotDocs

In law firms, the top three document assembly packages according to the ABA's 2018 Legal Technology Survey Report are HotDocs, ProLaw, and AIA Contract Documents. HotDocs (https://www.hotdocs.com/) is the most popular document assembly software by a large margin. HotDocs is a very powerful solution and has significantly matured over the years. HotDocs is composed of many different products, such as those used for template creation, cloud-based access, desktop template distribution, and centralized server-based distribution to the users. HotDocs Developer 11 is one of the most powerful platforms for document automation and allows you to convert word processing documents and PDF forms into document generation templates. You create a template and determine what text to include or exclude, depending on the answers entered by the user. This is the survey type entry that was described earlier. The presentation walks you through the questions to gather the data needed to generate the document. The current version supports Microsoft Word 2007, 2010, 2013, and 2016 and WordPerfect X4, X5, X6, and X7. HotDocs User 11 is the other desktop product that allows you to organize, access and run HotDocs templates. With HotDocs User, you select a particular template for a specific document. You are then presented with an interview in a way that is easy to understand and use.

As with other application software these days, HotDocs is available in a browser version too. The product, HotDocs Server 11, allows for document assembly using a standard web browser. This is particularly helpful for remote users and means you can deploy templates via the internet. HotDocs Server 11 must be deployed in conjunction with a web application.

HotDocs also has a SaaS (software as a service) offering, which extends the browser-based document generation to the small and midsized firm. The HotDocs Cloud Services provide on-demand document generation in any modern browser on any device from within the context of any standards-compliant web application capable of making web service calls. Cloud Services could be used by firms that need browser-based document generation, prefer a hosted (subscription-based) solution, and want to integrate HotDocs interviews into existing web applications. Like other HotDocs products, you'll need to contact HotDocs to get a quote.

A new offering in 2018 is HotDocs Hub. HotDocs Hub is a new module set that makes it easier than ever before to implement HotDocs, no matter what size organization you have. The HotDocs Hub comprises a suite of interconnected, extensible and configurable modules, including enhanced template storage and management, user management, document storage, answer management and user interface. Currently, only the HotDocs Template Hub is available, which contains user management and on premise web API. Additional modules are being developed and will be available in the future.

Pricing information isn't available on the HotDocs website. You must speak with a HotDocs representative to customize your document generation solution. We'll continue to say that we hate the lack of transparency when companies hide pricing information and make you contact them. A free 30-day trial for HotDocs is available by completing the form on the website.

ProLaw

ProLaw by Thomson Reuters Elite (http://www.elite.com/prolaw/) is an integrated software product designed to automate the practice of law, complete with the business functions of billing, accounting and other financial management. It is a complete package and combines case and matter management along with its document assembly features. ProLaw is targeted to mid-sized firms and no longer has an offering for the small firm attorney. The document assembly component can create custom forms and templates with drag and drop fields. It can automatically convert documents to PDF and create templates that easily merge with the elements from the ProLaw database. ProLaw's document assembly capability also integrates with Microsoft Word. Pricing for the system must be obtained directly from Elite. This is not a cheap alternative and requires some pretty hefty hardware to run with acceptable performance. In fairness, ProLaw is much, much more than a stand-alone document assembly product such as HotDocs so the cost comparison isn't apples to apples.

AIA Contract Documents

AIA Contract Documents (https://www.aiacontracts.org/) is a specialty package used for design and construction projects, so it's an excellent product for those dealing with construction law. The documents and forms are prepared by the AIA with the consensus of owners, contractors, attorneys, architects, engineers, and others. The AIA documents are intended for nationwide use and are not restricted to specific states. However, there are some documents that are specific to certain states such as the Kentucky Department of Education version of the Owner-Contractor Agreement, Stipulated Sum. The current offering is online only and is called ACD5. In September of 2018, there were 206 documents available in the library.

A single user license that allows for unlimited documents is $1,249.99 per year. You can reduce that cost to $949.99 if you are an AIA member. If you are a mid to large size law firm, the license options range from the single user cost of $1,249.99 up to $35,499.99 for a fifty-seat license with unlimited documents.

If you don't want to fork over the money for unlimited access, there are two single document options. The lowest cost option is the Basic single document package, where the legal language cannot be modified. Each document may be completed only once and saved as a PDF document. The cost for the Basic single document is $29.99 for non-members and $24.99 for AIA members. The other option is the Customized single document package, where the legal language is editable and the document can only be finalized once. The cost of the Customized single contract document is $79.99 for non-members and $59.99 for AIA members. Pricing for forms is different. A form that is not editable is $11.99 for nonmembers and $9.99 for AIA members. Customizable single page forms are $29.99 for non-members and $24.99 for AIA members. Customizable multi-page forms are $39.99 for non-members and $29.99 for AIA members.

Final Thoughts

HotDocs is the clear recommendation for solo and small firm lawyers wanting to embark on document assembly. As a generic package, it is very well suited for any type of law practice. HotDocs integrates with many document management and practice management packages. There are many choices for technical support, including HotDocs Wiki, HotDocs Forum, HotDocs Resource Center, and HotDocs Documentation. HotDocs resellers are the primary method for consulting and product acquisition.

CHAPTER SIXTEEN

Cloud Computing

Everybody is talking about the cloud—in the legal profession and elsewhere. You can't go a single week without there being some mention of a new cloud service offering. The really scary part is that many users don't know what it means to use cloud computing and believe that the weather affects the "cloud." That's not a joke—almost half of Americans believe that.

For our discussion purposes, the cloud is generally viewed as an external computing resource that is typically accessed via the internet. You can participate in cloud computing by putting your own equipment in a secure data center and accessing your data (and perhaps applications) via the internet. If you don't use your own equipment and software but elect to purchase applications through third parties, then you are using a SaaS (software as a service) solution. To make it easy to understand, imagine that you don't own a copy of Microsoft Office; you simply go to a site on the internet where you are, by subscription, allowed to use Office. The resulting data is held by the provider, not you. This is exactly the environment that Microsoft is pushing with its extraordinarily successful Office 365 product.

Stats from the ABA Legal Technology Survey 2018 Report:

- A web-based software and service/cloud computing was used by 55 percent (compared to 52 percent in 2017, 38 percent in 2016, and 31 percent in 2015).
- Small firms (two to nine attorneys) were the most likely to respond affirmatively at 58 percent
- Those who had not used cloud computing (33 percent) cited the following factors preventing them from using cloud computing:
  - 56 percent: Confidentiality and security concerns
  - 49 percent: Lack of control over data
  - 39 percent: Unfamiliarity with the technology
  - 19 percent: Cost/effort of switching from your current solution
  - 19 percent: Cost of services
  - 16 percent: Lack of control regarding software upgrades
  - 15 percent: Uncertainty over longevity of vendor

- 14 percent: Client concerns about firm using cloud
- 7 percent: Lack of reliable internet connection
- 6 percent: Lack of desired or necessary features
- 5 percent: Lack of integrations
- 5 percent: Vendor turning data over to law enforcement
- 5 percent: Other

The traditional client/server model puts total control in the hands of the law firm. The data is held internally, and access is controlled by the firm. You can choose to encrypt the data locally, which we recommend, or leave it in plain text. Either way, it is within the technology walls of the law firm and not directly accessible by any third party.

In contrast, the SaaS model puts your data in the hands of a third party. This is not necessarily a bad thing, but do you really know if the information is safe? Your contract with the provider may specify that the data be stored in encrypted form, but what if a disgruntled employee has access to tools that allow him or her to decrypt the data and sell it to the other side in a major lawsuit? An ongoing concern for lawyers, in light of the Edward Snowden revelations and NSA capabilities, is whether there is (or will be in the future) a government "back door" that allows it access to your data.

When you contract with a SaaS provider, you are required to accept the service as it is delivered to you. This means any upgrades or bug fixes will be implemented by the provider. Sound like a good thing? Perhaps not. What if the upgrade breaks integration with another product that you use? As you can see above, 16 percent of respondents cited lack of control regarding software upgrades as a reason to avoid the cloud.

Besides the data security and access concerns for the SaaS model, the financial stability of the provider may be a consideration, but it is becoming less of an issue as more and more vendors are providing cloud solutions. Still, 15 percent of respondents to the 2018 Legal Technology Survey are concerned about the longevity of the vendor. Even if you have adequate notice that the vendor will stop providing a contracted service, the cost to migrate your data to another provider or bring it back in-house can be significant. This brings us to the topic of exit strategy. At some point, you may want to bring the function back within your IT control or move to another provider.

The contract should provide for specific costs and timetables to facilitate the move. It should also specify what file format you will get your data in. Will you get a copy of the complete SQL database along with the schema or just a comma delimited text file?

Another issue is the stability of the communications network. By design, you are dependent on the speed and quality of your internet connection. Smart firms will have dual network connections to the internet, although this will mean an increase in cost over what is normally installed at the firm. The internet connection must be available at all times; otherwise, you will not have access to your data. There aren't many judges who are sympathetic to your problems if you miss a filing date because your internet connection went down and you couldn't get to your data. And internet connections, as we've all miserably learned, do sometimes go down—and always without notice. Some providers do offer a local copy of the data that synchronizes with the cloud copy. That way you can work offline and the data will synchronize back to the provider once you are connected to the internet.

Finally, there is the issue of access to your data. Is the vendor scanning your data for marketing purposes? Some vendors do exactly that so they can serve up targeted ads. Does the vendor give third-party access to your data? There was a huge backlash when it was revealed that Facebook was allowing Cambridge Analytica access to the personally identifiable information of millions of Facebook users. Make sure you know what measures the cloud provider has in place to prevent unauthorized access to client confidential data.

To be fair, let's look at the upsides of using the cloud and yes, there are some compelling upsides.

There can be some financial advantages to contracting service to a third-party provider. Your investment in hardware and software is minimized, since you are really only passing keyboard, mouse, and screen data over the communications link or typically accessing the application via a web browser. The actual processing occurs at the cloud provider. All configuration and data hosting are external to your firm's infrastructure. Costs for the SaaS model can be based on the number of users or the amount of data storage volume. Either way, it is fairly easy to identify and budget for the cost of the service, which is a big selling point for a lot of firms. However, to get these "stable" price points, the contract terms are typically several years. This means that the firm must make a pretty long commitment to using the SaaS model and the specific provider.

The alternative to the long contract term is a much shorter subscription model. Many cloud service providers are now providing solutions where you have to commit to an annual subscription. Some are even offering month-to-month subscriptions. Typically, the shorter the commitment period, the higher the cost per month. As an example, many cloud-based case management applications won't make you commit to more than a year.

Another advantage to the SaaS model is the rapid reaction time to changes. It is very fast to add new users or to increase the amount of space for data storage. By the same measure, it is very fast to decrease the number of users or amount of storage space. This means that you are more flexible in controlling your costs. If your firm is in contraction mode, you can reduce expenses, assuming that the contract doesn't tie you to a minimum amount. Many firms like the mobility aspect of the cloud model, since they can access the applications from any machine with an internet browser. Typically, there isn't anything special that needs to be installed on the client computer. The user needs only a browser and perhaps some type of plug-in to access the application. This means that it is easy to gain access to the firm's data from the office, the home, or an internet café in the Bahamas.

Too often, all costs and all risks are not considered when analyzing a cloud solution. The cloud ballyhoo has drowned out all reasonable objections. We originally moved slowly and carefully in moving clients to cloud solutions, but we do understand that some cloud services make sense for the solo and small firm attorney. More on that later. Client/server solutions can be clearly defined from implementation through the life of the solution. You control the implementation, configuration, and ongoing costs. While you can contractually specify some costs with a cloud provider, future upgrades and exit conversions may tip the financial decision.

You may also hear of two other cloud solutions. Platform as a Service (PaaS) and Infrastructure as a Service (IaaS) are two additional cloud computing services. With PaaS, the client creates software using features and capabilities as available from the provider. Most law firms will not entertain the PaaS model. With IaaS, the necessary infrastructure is supplied by the solution provider. It owns and controls the equipment, operating system, network, and so on, and you load your applications onto the services. Think of it as having your data and applications running on "rented" hardware.

Contract Considerations

Now for a show of hands. How many readers have actually read the terms of service or terms and conditions for a cloud provider service? When we ask that question at continuing legal education programs, you could count the number of raised hands with the fingers on one hand. Shame, shame, shame. As lawyers, you should be reading the contracts and the terms that you are agreeing to. Fear not. We'll point out some of the items and considerations you should be looking for in contracts with service providers.

Where will the data reside? Will it be in the United States or in some foreign country? Can you specify where the data will reside? Certainly, we would recommend that the data remain in the United States, which would avoid any cross-border issues and having to deal with international laws. And yes, even with the Snowden revelations, we don't want data in privacy-focused Europe where we don't know the laws and would potentially need a European lawyer to help in the event of a problem. "Better the devil you know," as we say ruefully.

- Is the data encrypted in storage and in transmission? Encryption will help protect the confidentiality of the information. The majority of cloud providers will encrypt the data in transit (e.g., SSL/TLS connections), but not necessarily at rest while it sits on their servers.
- Who controls the encryption keys, and is there a master decryption key? Just because the data is encrypted doesn't mean it is accessible only to you. Services like Dropbox encrypt the data in transit and while it is stored on their servers; however, they hold a master decryption key and have the ability to decrypt your data. Services like Spider Oak allow you to define the encryption passphrase, and they have no master decryption key. The good news is that there exists technology where the end user controls the encryption key and not the service provider.
- Who can access your data? This may not matter if you control the encryption, but it is worth knowing your exposure.
- What is the exit strategy? Is there a cost? What form will the data be in? How long will it take to get your data? You certainly don't want to be held hostage by the vendor when trying to leave its service.
- Who owns the data? It seems like it should be a silly question, but is the data really yours or can the provider access it and redistribute it?
- What about data breaches? Make sure you understand who is responsible should there be a data breach. Who makes and pays for the data breach notifications? Will the cloud provider pay for any identity theft monitoring if required? Does the provider have adequate cyberinsurance coverage?
- Is your data stored on separate physical devices, or are you comingled with other cloud customers? Comingled storage puts you at risk should the authorities want to seize equipment for a cloud customer that you share storage with. Think of the Megaupload situation, in which many businesses went bankrupt when the authorities seized servers in a criminal investigation and their data was commingled with the company being investigated.

Private Cloud Solution

We think that moving your data and applications to a secure data center is a much better solution for most solo and small firm lawyers. Think of it as the best of all worlds. It's your data and software running on equipment that you own and control. If you don't like the data center, you can always move or bring it back in-house. The costs are even more predictable because you control any upgrades.

We have purchased rack space at data centers over the last several years and moved our clients' equipment into the secured racks. Not so long ago, weather conditions in our area (a massive snowfall and a drenching storm that had folks without power for weeks) made more firms cognizant of business continuity solutions. Data centers have redundant power (generators too) and internet connections. This means that weather conditions will not affect your ability to access your data and applications. Data centers generally guarantee at least 99.999 percent (called the five nines) uptime. Remember, though, that your own equipment could fail and you are still dependent on your local internet connection. However, if your power in the office and at home is down, you can drive (as one of our clients did) to a Starbucks a few miles away and be back in business using a VPN.

As you engineer the architecture to implement a private cloud (some may call it a hybrid solution), be particularly aware of any software applications that contain databases such as your case management software. Database access using the internet as the network is extremely risky and will typically result in corrupted data. You may have to implement a terminal server–type connection so that you run the client software from equipment at the data center instead of "dragging" all the data between your computer and the server over the internet. Your IT consultant can help you determine the right connection scheme for each of your applications to achieve the greatest stability for your needs.

Bottom line: Although we don't regret our initial caution with moving law firms to the cloud, we feel we have now solved most potential problems and that the law firms can feel comfortable that they are complying with ethical requirements when storing confidential data in the cloud. We are now actively moving more and more clients to the cloud, though using the client's hardware rather than the cloud provider's. If you feel that you need to investigate and research SaaS vendors, we describe a few in this book. We just ask that you do it carefully and ask the right questions before making your decision.

We believe that most cloud providers actually offer better security than law firms themselves. We are therefore moving in the direction of recommending cloud solutions from proven providers with good track records. It is particularly helpful if the cloud provider has experience with serving legal entities.

Finally, be sure to check with your bar, as a number of states now have ethics opinions regarding cloud computing. If you're wondering how states are dealing with the cloud from an ethical perspective, the general view is that it is acceptable to use the cloud as long as you investigate the provider, particularly making sure that confidential client data will be adequately protected. An excellent resource is provided (free of charge) by the Legal Technology Resource Center of the American Bar Association available at https://www.americanbar.org/groups/departments_offices/legal_technology_resources/resources/charts_fyis/cloud-ethics-chart.html, where you will find a list of cloud ethics opinions for the various states. Remember that, ethically, you are outsourcing when you contract with a cloud provider, so the ethical rules relating to outsourcing also apply.

On March 17, 2016, the Legal Cloud Computing Association released the first set of cloud security standards crafted specifically for the legal industry at ABA TECHSHOW. It is a short document containing 21 standards—and easy to read. You can review the document at http://www.legalcloudcomputingassociation.org/standards. We thought it was pretty ironic that a document addressing cloud security doesn't use a secure https:// connection.

CHAPTER SEVENTEEN

Collaboration

Collaboration may or may not be at the top of your list, especially if you are a solo lawyer. However, we're sure you will have occasion to deal with other lawyers or even have a need to collaborate with your clients on a case. There are some great technology solutions that allow for collaboration—and solutions are multiplying week by week. These are just a few of the primary tools available for sharing information and working in a collaborative mode.

Social networking is a collaboration area that is gaining in popularity. Facebook has won the social networking war and is now being used extensively for business purposes. Though as we write this edition, Facebook has taken an enormous nosedive after numerous admissions involving betraying the privacy of users. But it is still the leader of the pack, bruised though it may be. Twitter and LinkedIn are also very popular, with many lawyers preferring LinkedIn as a network for professionals. Some lawyers are getting business through social media sites, and others are raising their visibility with potential clients or colleagues who might provide referrals. Still others have obtained opportunities to write or speak on their area of expertise.

We're also seeing an increase in collaboration with clients by using client portals with cloud service providers. More and more of the case management vendors have client portals so that clients can collaborate securely with their attorneys and even gain access to documents and other information for their matter. Clients are much more in tune with their lawyers when they use a client portal. They know what issues are pending, tasks that are completed and the financial status (e.g. invoice, retainer amount, etc.) of their matter.

Portals are an excellent way for lawyers to collaborate with clients. Document collaboration is probably the biggest focus for many lawyers. The number one tool for document collaboration used among lawyers is Citrix ShareFile. We're also seeing a larger move towards collaborative communications using tools like Slack and Teams.

Considerations

We won't go into a lot of details concerning the options for collaboration. There is an excellent book which is available from the ABA by Law Practice Division members Tom Mighell and Dennis Kennedy called *The Lawyer's Guide to Collaboration Tools and Technologies, 2nd Edition*, which dives into great detail on all sorts of collaboration tools. We couldn't do it justice with just a few pages here.

At a high level, there are several considerations when choosing a collaboration method or tool. Does something already exist in a product you already own? As an example, perhaps your practice management software has a client portal. You can collaborate with your client or co-counsel using the portal. If you are an Office 365 user, does your subscription include Microsoft SharePoint or Teams? How many people need to collaborate concurrently? Are there free tools (e.g. Skype) that are "good enough" for your needs? Do you need to carry on a "conversation" or is file sharing all you need? When collaborating on a document, are all revisions pre-served? You probably need some method of securing or limiting access to information as well.

There are a lot of collaboration options. Get Dennis and Tom's book. You won't be disappointed.

CHAPTER EIGHTEEN

Remote Access

Most lawyers today are road warriors. If their entire office is not on a laptop or smartphone, a good chunk of it is—and the rest is accessible through remote access. Whether in court, on vacation, on the road, or in a meeting, lawyers need access to their email, calendar, appointments, and files—and they need access fast.

Many lawyers have discarded workstations entirely, using only their laptop and a docking station at work and tablets and smartphones while on the move. Others have both a workstation and a laptop. The popularity of laptops and other mobile devices has zoomed in the last decade, to the point where the lawyer without a laptop or smartphone is a rarity. Our new mobile lawyers are now equipped with technologies that allow them to be as productive on the road as they are in the office, minimizing downtime and keeping those billable hours (or productivity hours, in the case of the alternative billers) up. Many clients and colleagues have a strong expectation that lawyers will be constantly accessible via email—even, sadly, while on vacation. We privately joke (and lament) that vacations are times when our mobile devices get a nice view of the beach. Many clients will disregard your out-of-office message and will expect a quick response. So how do we stay in touch with the office when on the road?

Virtual Private Networking

A virtual private network (VPN) connection is a secure communications network tunneled through another network such as the internet. The VPN connection allows a user to connect to the office when working remotely. The communications tunnel encrypts the data traffic between the remote user and the office network, maintaining the security of the information as it is passed back and forth. This is extremely important for law firms whose lawyers work on client files while traveling or while away from the office and have to download a local copy of a client file to work on. Best of all, the

VPN service software is included with Microsoft's server operating systems and the VPN client software is included with Microsoft operating systems at no additional cost to the user.

The average lawyer is likely to be dumbfounded when confronted with setting up a VPN, especially if third-party software and a certificate are required, so this is best left to your IT consultant. However, it is not terribly expensive, and it offers terrific security for your data. The greatest advantage of VPNs is that they are multiuser, whereas other methods are one-on-one solutions.

If you're traveling and don't have access or the ability to create a mobile hotspot—which is the preferred, secure way of accessing the internet when traveling, you should always fall back on a VPN. A VPN service such as VPN Unlimited (www.vpnunlimitedapp.com) allows users to create an encrypted connection to the internet, which is important if you're planning on using the "open" wireless network at your next legal conference or meeting. This app can be installed on your mobile device or computer system, and allows for complete anonymous, secure internet access. This subscription service is available in packages for purchase in as a single month, several months or years, and even a lifetime package that never expires. The pricing ranges from $9.99 for one month to $199.99 for the lifetime subscription, and is one that the authors use on a regular basis when traveling.

If you are confused as to which VPN service you should use, a resource that compares 185 VPNs is available at https://thatoneprivacysite.net/. The comparisons help you determine what features are most important to you. Does the provider log information about your connection? Is the pricing reasonable? What is the security level? The charts are in easy-to-understand color codes, where green means good.

GoToMyPC

GoToMyPC is a remote connection service that allows you to connect to your work computer when you are away from the office. This service is a great alternative if you're a solo practitioner or if your law firm does not have the ability to set up a VPN-type connection for remote users (for example, if you don't have a server). Like a VPN connection, data communications between the client and the host are encrypted and secured. To connect to your work computer, software must be installed and running on the host machine (the computer you wish to connect to), and both the client and the host computers must have internet access. The GoToMyPC website maintains contact with the host computer, so the IP address of the host is always known. This is critical: This solution works even if the host has a dynamic internet connection (constantly changing IP address) instead of a static one, which remains constant. No modifications to the configuration of your firm firewall will need to be made to get GoToMyPC up and running.

Users can even connect to their work computers (Mac or Windows) from a tablet or smartphone. Apps are available for Android, iOS, and Kindle Fire devices.

GoToMyPC costs as little as $35 per month for one computer license when billed annually. There is no limitation on how often you may connect to your host computer, and you are allowed to connect to your host computer from any device. The Pro plan includes the ability to remotely connect to two different systems. The software requires little setup and configuration and can be purchased online from GoToMyPC's website at www.gotomypc.com. This software is more costly than its competitors, so be sure to check out all of your available options before selecting which remote access solution to purchase. GoToMyPC also has a seven-day free trial, so take advantage as you experiment to find which remote access solution works best for you!

LogMeIn

LogMeIn Pro is a remote access solution that is very similar to GoToMyPC. The software works the exact same way, with the service provider maintaining the IP addresses of host computers. This is another good solution for those firms with dynamic (constantly changing) IP addresses. With this service and very little effort, you can gain seamless and total access to your office PC (Mac or Windows) from any computer with an internet connection. To connect, a user logs in to the LogMeIn website (or uses the app downloaded to her mobile device) and the connection to the host computer is made automatically. Some of the features include remote printing, the ability to transfer and share files between the connected computers, and the ability to map network drives to your local computer. Just like GoToMyPC, this service is extremely secure, using 128-bit to 256-bit SSL end-to-end encryption. Compared to GoToMyPC ($420 when billed annually), this remote access solution is slightly lower at $349.99 per year, and allows a user to access up to two different computers as well.

This service also supports connecting to your work computer from your iOS or Android device. We've used the iPad app, and it works as advertised—easy to use, great with the touchscreen, and very convenient.

A LogMeIn Pro subscription will need to be renewed annually. This service can be purchased online from LogMeIn's website at https://store.logmein.com. We strongly recommend the use of this product for remote accessibility because of its ease of use and ability to access two computers instead of just one. LogMeIn offers a 14-day free trial, so we recommend taking the product for a test drive before purchasing it.

TeamViewer

TeamViewer Business Edition is a remote access solution on steroids. It contains a number of features that are not available with LogMeIn or GoToMyPC. Although it's a onetime purchase, it comes with a hefty price. Just like the two remote access solutions described above, TeamViewer works flawlessly behind network firewalls and is a good solution for firms that use dynamic IP addresses. While TeamViewer is not difficult to install and run, the connecting computer will need to download, install, and run the client application, which, in our experience, may be a bit more confusing and cumbersome for lawyers to perform rather than just logging in to the service with the web browser.

Mobile device support is available for iOS, Android, and Windows 10 Mobile in all subscription plan levels. TeamViewer Business is available online from www.teamviewer.com, and a single business license for a single user costs $49 per month or $588 per year. This version permits connections to an unlimited number of endpoints (e.g. computer or mobile devices).

Mobility Tips

Besides providing remote access solutions for the legal road warrior, we wanted to include some useful tips to think about before heading out on the road:

- Pack a surge protector. It doesn't matter what brand. You never know when you will need more than two outlets to power all of your devices and to protect your electronic devices from power surges and dirty electricity.
- Purchase a lock for your laptop. Ninety-nine percent of laptops have a Kensington security slot, and it's prudent to use it. Kensington

locks, such as the MicroSaver DS Notebook Lock, are available online from Kensington's website (www.kensington.com) for around $55—a small price to pay to keep your laptop secure.

- If you use a wireless Bluetooth mouse, be sure to pack extra AA or AAA batteries.
- Pack a spare cell phone charger and tablet charger with an extra sync cable. You shouldn't travel without either one.
- Pack an AC extension cable. This will come in handy when you are far away from a power outlet.
- Keep an AC power adapter for your laptop in your bag. You never know when you might need one.
- It is always a good idea to have a hard copy printout of your hotel reservation and itinerary, in the event your mobile device stops working or isn't accessible when you need it. If you are using your mobile device to keep track of your itinerary, try using an app like TripIt, which can track all your travel arrangements, including your flights, hotel, and rental car information, and will eliminate the searching of your email for your travel plans. How nice is it to have all of the information in a single place? Plus, another great feature is that this app allows you to share your itinerary with family and friends.
- Keep appropriate video adapters with your laptop in your laptop bag. You never know when you might need to connect your laptop or tablet to a TV or projector for a presentation.
- Pack headphones to keep the noise out. Have you ever tried to be productive on an airplane? It's hard when the person next to you can't stop talking. Just plug in your headphones and your problem is solved. You can even listen to relaxing music while you work. For those who want wireless Bluetooth headphones, check out the Jabra Elite Sport, costing about $220, which can be found on Jabra's website at www.jabra.com; however, you won't be able to use these during takeoff and landing because they are transmitting devices. For music aficionados, the Bose QuietComfort 35 wireless headphones II offer top-of-the-line headphone technology and include the noise-canceling circuitry that you hear everyone talking about. The downside, though, is the price—very, very expensive at around $350. The authors are particularly fond of the Bose QC 20 earbuds. They are small and lightweight and have amazingly effective noise-canceling capability. However, they are also pricey at $249.95.
- Back up your data to an external hard drive or the network server. If your laptop crashes or is stolen, you will want a recent backup of your most important files.
- Encrypt your hard drive and data. There are many software tools available to do this, such as Symantec Drive Encryption and Folder

Lock. In the event your laptop is lost or stolen, your data is protected. Configure a power on or BIOS password on your computer, if available. Again, this adds another layer of data protection.

- If you have a tablet, be sure to password-protect your device with a passphrase. PINs aren't as secure and can be easily cracked. On an iPad, a passphrase requirement on the Lock Screen will enable encryption of your data. On Android devices, you can encrypt your data as well by using a lock code or through the configuration settings for older OS versions.
- If you have a smartphone with a data plan that allows device tethering or a mobile hot spot, take advantage of the data service you have already paid for and create a hot spot for your laptop or tablet with your smartphone for internet service. Avoid paying daily hotel fees for an internet connection if it's not provided free during the course of your stay. However, data overage charges from your wireless carrier can be expensive, so it's best not to stream the movie at the top of your Netflix queue while tethered unless you truly have an unlimited data plan.
- Encrypt your USB flash drives and external hard drives.
- Disable your wireless auto-connection feature within the Windows operating system. Most laptops with wireless cards will automatically connect to any unencrypted, open wireless network when your default connection is unavailable. If by chance your device does connect to an open wireless network, never log in to any email or bank account when using an unsecure connection. Hopefully, we all will be using WPA3 connections for public networks in the near future.
- Before leaving the office, make sure that your security software has the latest updates and definitions to protect your devices while you're away. The same applies to Windows updates.
- Download and install an app to track your club membership cards so that you don't have to carry all that plastic around with you. The one that we like the most for iOS and Android mobile devices is the Key Ring Rewards Cards app. It not only allows you to enter and store your club card or membership numbers but also generates a bar code that can be scanned should one be required. You might as well get miles points and hotel rewards while on the go.
- Another great app to download and use on your mobile device is GateGuru. This app comes in handy when your flight has been canceled or delayed, and you're looking to kill a few hours. This app provides maps of all major airport terminals, including restaurants and stores, along with reviews allowing you to find a bar or restaurant in which to relax and unwind until your flight.

- For Android users, Google's Wi-Fi Assistant app uses free and available hotspots to connect your mobile device to the internet. It also secures your data through the usage of VPN service managed by Google. Free, secure Wi-Fi sounds like a great idea and reduces carrier data usage at the same time!

Here are some tips when traveling abroad:

- If you travel abroad, you also have to worry about foreign governments—and our own—which may be interested in your data. Lawyers are not only not exempt from that interest—they are magnets. The advice is generally applicable to the risks presented by foreign governments, risks which may increase as there seems to be a worldwide ratcheting up of device seizure and examination at borders.
- U.S. citizens are not required to unlock their phones or share passwords with U.S. government officials. However, rules may vary depending on where you are traveling to and from. But being detained and intimidated is not an experience any traveler wants to go through.
- Travel with a "burner" (disposable) phone and clean tablet or laptop. If you use your regular smartphone, we recommend that you disable fingerprint readers because, in the U.S., law enforcement agencies can use warrants to compel you to unlock your phone with your fingerprint. We would go further and advise disabling all biometrics used to get into your phone, such as iris scans and facial recognition.
- Whenever you travel, use a password manager to "remember" all of your passwords. Don't have the password management software loaded on your devices. It is best to store the password vault (encrypted of course) in a cloud service like Dropbox and get access to it when you reach your destination.
- Protect your social media and email accounts by having two-factor authentication enabled—assuming you have left your phone at home. Since the text code will be sent to that phone, officials will be unable to get into your accounts even with your password.
- When dealing with email, do not install and configure any email client on your laptop or cell phone. You don't want to have any email on your devices. You should use some sort of remote access solution (e.g. Citrix, LogMeIn, etc.) to access your email. Even using a browser could leave remnants of confidential information on your device.
- Any device you use while abroad should be encrypted. The best way to ensure that your data remains secure is to back up your data to a cloud service and then wipe all of your devices before you return home. Once home, you can restore your data from the backup.

- No matter what device you use abroad, assume that all electronic communication is subject to interception. This means you should always be using a secure encrypted connection. Make sure you have a properly configured VPN available and know how to use it.
- Another tip for international travelers: Leave your cell phone at home. Roaming charges can be staggering and can be initiated even if you're not actively using your phone. Do you really trust putting your phone in airplane mode?
- Be sure to pack multiple converters so that you can connect your devices. In the United States, we operate on a system that runs at 120 volts. Be sure to check the voltage of the country you're visiting before leaving and find out whether your power supplies will auto-convert. You may not need voltage convertors if the power supplies auto-adjust, but you will need the plug adapters to match the outlet connections.
- One point to note, however, is that if you're traveling internationally, encryption is illegal in some countries, which could lead to the confiscation of your encrypted devices—so be prepared and know the local laws. In some cases, it may make more sense to leave your data at home and connect remotely to your system to access your information, rather than to take it with you.

These are just a few of the recommendations we have for the legal road warriors, all based on our own experiences traveling. We hope you find them useful.

CHAPTER NINETEEN

Mobile Security

Technology advances in this area have come at warp speed. We're old enough to remember when dialup was the only way you could connect to the internet and cellular phones were almost as big as a briefcase. We can't remember the last time we even saw a modem as an option when configuring a laptop purchase. Wireless, whether using Wi-Fi or a 3G/4G data connection with your cellular carrier, is the preferred method of connectivity in the modern age. More and more hotels, motels, conference centers, coffee shops, bookstores, cafés, and so on, are offering wireless access solutions, many without charge. The question is . . . should you use the free Wi-Fi?

Security Software

Before we jump into the boring details, let's cover some solutions that should be on your laptop no matter what other technology you use for remote connectivity. It goes without saying that you should have some sort of all-in-one security solution installed on your laptop. It should be configured to check for automatic updates and to perform a periodic full scan (weekly scans would be good) to catch anything that may have "landed" before the signatures were updated. It would be just your luck to catch a virus or other malware on day one and be the first kid on the block to suffer the effects.

Most of the current internet suites also analyze the computer operation and identify activity that could be malwarelike or some process trying to access something it shouldn't. This type of real-time monitoring provides added protection beyond mere signature files. Normally, the all-in-one security product will contain security features like antivirus, anti-malware, firewalls, spam control, anti-phishing, etc. Some products also include some form of artificial intelligence (AI). The products continue to improve so don't leave home without them. Software solutions for your smartphone and tablet are also available, but we'll discuss those later.

Encryption

Secure mobile computing must contain some method of encryption to protect valuable personal and client data. We prefer whole disk encryption. This means everything on the hard drive is encrypted and kept secure. We don't have to remember to put files into special folders or on the encrypted virtual drive. All too often, people are in a big hurry and may not save their data in the special protected encrypted areas, leaving the information vulnerable. With whole disk encryption you don't have to think. Save the data anywhere on the drive and it's protected.

In addition, without whole disk encryption, artifacts of the decryption passphrase could be present in various places (e.g., master file table, Page File, temp files, unallocated space). Forensics can extract these artifacts and make it probable that the passphrase can be determined. Many of the newer laptops have built-in whole disk encryption. To state the obvious, make sure you enable the encryption; otherwise, your data won't be protected. Windows 10 Professional includes BitLocker encryption for free. Mac users can take advantage of File Vault 2, which is also included free of charge. Encryption software from vendors such as Symantec, Trend Micro, and Check Point are also good choices. In addition, encryption may be used in conjunction with biometric access. As an example, our laptops require a fingerprint when powered on. Failure at that point leaves the computer hard drive fully encrypted. A very comforting thought if laptop thieves, who constitute a large club these days, make off with your laptop.

If encryption in all its many varieties is your particular interest, a much more expansive resource on encryption is the book *Encryption Made Simple for Lawyers* (authored by Sharon Nelson, David Ries, and John Simek) and available from the ABA web store.

Wireless

Wireless is the norm for all the road warriors. There are two basic types of wireless access you'll encounter. The first type is generically termed a "wireless hot spot" and is what you find at your local Starbucks, fast-food establishment, hotel, or airport. You may or may not have to pay for these wireless connection services. Many businesses are offering free wireless as a way to attract customers—heck, even McDonald's offers a free wireless hot spot. Most of these hot spots are unsecured and wide open. This means it is possible for your confidential data to be viewed by the customer at the next table or the person sitting on the park bench outside the café if you are not encrypting the traffic.

Does this mean you shouldn't use any of these wireless networks? If you have a choice, we would say these networks are best avoided by those who are technology averse and don't understand how to operate securely in an unsecured environment. Read on and determine whether you can safely be trusted to do what follows.

See if there is an option to have a secure connection to the Wi-Fi network. This would be indicated if you use https:// (note the s, denoting "secure") as part of the URL. Typically, website connections are unsecure and do not provide an encrypted session like the https:// connections do, but that is changing quickly. Modern browsers are enforcing encryption and will begin blocking websites that aren't https://.

Be especially careful if you have to pay for the wireless connection. Be wary when you are at the screens that have you input your credit card and billing information. Do not enter any of this sensitive information without an https:// connection. Once you've established a connection to the wireless network, be sure to use your VPN or other secure (https://) access to protect your transmissions. Also, when connecting to a secure website, if you're presented with an error message referencing a SSL certificate error or invalid certificate, proceed with extreme caution or, better yet, don't proceed at all. The good news is that more and more browsers are helping to limit access to insecure sites. Chrome is especially aggressive in this area.

Some hotels may give you a wireless network that is already secured. Typically, these wireless implementations use WPA (Wi-Fi protected access) or WPA2 to secure your connection and data. The network will be visible to your computer, but you will be required to provide a password before your computer connects. Once connected, the data you transmit will be encrypted and secure. However, know that WEP (wired equivalent privacy) and WPA have both been cracked. This means they are insecure methods of encryption.

Last year, it was discovered that the WPA2 protocol is vulnerable as well. The vulnerability is exploited by using key reinstallation attacks (KRACKs). It primarily attacks the Wi-Fi client. Vendors have patches available for the vulnerability so make sure you have applied them. Even if you are using an encrypted Wi-Fi network such as WPA2, typically it will be configured with a pre-shared key (PSK). This mean that every connection uses the same password and encryption key. If you know the password, you can potentially eavesdrop on others connected to the same Wi-Fi network. Even though there are known weaknesses in WPA2, you should only be connected to and using WPA2 Wi-Fi networks for secure wireless communications.

The good news is that WPA3 is coming. The specification has been finalized and several Wi-Fi chipsets have been certified. Vendors are now in the process of incorporating the WPA3 specification into new products. As we write, WPA3 products are expected to appear late in 2018 with full scale consumer availability by the end of 2019. One of the key features of WPA3 is in securing public Wi-Fi networks such as those found in common public areas. Instead of users using a pre-shared key, a unique key will be generated for each connection. That means you won't be able to "sniff" the traffic of someone else connected to the same network as you can with WPA2. Make sure you budget for an equipment upgrade to WPA3 in 2019.

One scheme we see all the time: You are in a hotel that requires you to pay for internet access. But when you ask your computer to show "all available wireless networks," it will display something like "free public wireless" as a network name—or something else that sounds innocuous, usually using the word "free" to entice you. Beware—these are often data thieves offering up an insecure cloud for the sole purpose of making off with your data. You can get the "free internet"—but at a terrible price. Never be tempted by these clouds.

Public Computer Usage

A word of warning here. Be very careful about using a public computer, such as those in a library, an internet café, or the business center of a hotel. Even if you are only accessing your web-based email account, some data is temporarily written to the local hard disk. There is also the risk that some keystroke logging software is installed on the computer, thereby capturing everything that you do on the machine. Studies have shown an average of seven pieces of malware on these public computers.

Does that mean all public computers are off limits? Not at all. Just don't do anything on the computer that would reveal your identity or expose private information. Even using a hotel business center computer to print your boarding pass would reveal your airline user ID and password, potentially risking the theft of your airline miles. Another reason to travel with your own equipment.

Smartphones

Want to know what the most secure smartphone on the market is? Although we are asked that question a lot, that really isn't the right question. The question should be: What smartphone can be made the most secure? The answer is an Android phone. Because of its design architecture, Android can be configured with enhanced security settings as well as installing security software to protect the OS.

Having said that, both Android and iOS devices have greatly improved security over the years, even in default configurations. As for the iPhone, it was first designed as a consumer device, with security an afterthought. However, the latest versions of iOS on the newer iPhones have significantly improved security, especially when it comes to putting control of encryption in the users' hands. Apple still holds control of the operating system kernel and provides very limited access to developers in accessing more core functions of the operating system. This means that third-party developers finally have an opportunity to produce software that can further increase the security of the iPhone, iPad, and so on. With each new version of hardware and iOS, Apple is clamping down on the privacy issues and encrypting more and more information that is stored on the device. Modern iPhones and Android devices are encrypted by default when locked by a PIN, password or biometric, but remember that a court (at least in a civil case) may order you to turn over "the key" to your device.

At a minimum, everybody should have a PIN code programmed into their phone to prevent unauthorized access, along with a fairly short time-out period. It doesn't do much good to have an unlocking PIN and then have 30 minutes pass before the phone relocks. We know it's a pain to constantly punch in the unlock code, but that will keep your data from being accessed by prying eyes. Better yet, it will stop someone from installing spyware on your phone that can effectively trap all of your communications (voice calls, email, text messages, etc.) and send them elsewhere. For those devices that offer a passphrase alternative to the PIN, such as the iPad or iPhone, this would be the preferred choice to secure your device. Why, you might ask?

A passphrase can be longer than a PIN and can contain nonnumeric values, vastly increasing the strength of the protection. In fact, we do not recommend that any iPhone or iPad be configured with the very weak default six-digit PIN lock code. There are now devices and software specifically designed to bypass a lock code on an iPhone.

Encrypt the phone! This is easier to do than you think. Enabling a lock code on the iPhone or iPad automatically encrypts the device. The latest several versions of the Android operating system have built-in encryption as well. The later versions of Android work just like an iPhone. Configure a password or PIN (or biometric) lock and the device is encrypted. Android has had built-in encryption for some time now. Actually, if you are running an older version of Android that doesn't have built-in encryption, it's well past time for you to replace the phone. There are significant security vulnerabilities in the older versions of Android and iOS. You really don't have much to worry about if you are using the latest versions of iOS or Android devices since they are encrypted by default.

Besides PIN-protecting your phone, make sure you encrypt any memory cards or just don't store any sensitive data on them. We're talking about the SD, micro SD, and similar cards that you can insert into the smartphone to increase storage capacity. Again, the later versions of Android allow you to encrypt the card by checking a box in the settings. The point is, you don't want any confidential information to be accessible on the card if you lose your phone. The PIN will protect the phone access, but the "bad guy" will pop out the memory card and read it from his/her computer if it is not encrypted. iPhone users don't have to worry about this since memory expansion is not an option.

You should also have security software installed on your device no matter what operating system is running. Despite what some Apple "geniuses" say, Apple products are just as vulnerable as other products and require security software. Apple itself says the same thing. The antivirus software you use on your computers probably has versions for your smartphones too. This means you can centrally manage all your computers and mobile devices too. As an alternative, we recommend you investigate security software from Lookout, Trend Micro, or Sophos.

Finally, make sure you know how to wipe the data from the smartphone remotely if it is lost. You should have the phone configured to wipe automatically after a set number of invalid unlock attempts. This will clear the data even if you are not connected to a cellular network. Remotely wiping the device on demand requires that it be in communication with the cellular data network. Configure the "Find my iPhone" function within the iCloud settings on an iPhone or iPad. Use the Android Device Manager (https://www.google.com/android/find) that will help users locate or remotely wipe their phone. You must enable Android Device Manager from the Google settings on your phone and associate the phone with your Google account. Remember that the remote wipe feature is for the memory within the phone itself and may not wipe the memory cards we spoke about earlier.

iPhone users need to be particularly sensitive about their iCloud credentials. Many users share their iCloud account with family members and associate multiple devices to the account. That's a good and bad thing. One of the features users love is the automatic synchronization of data across multiple Apple devices. This is achieved by registering your device with an iCloud account. This hardly makes it private if you share your iCloud credentials with others. We see the abuse of this feature quite a bit in family law matters. Spouses forget that data is synchronized between devices, thereby making it available to another party. Sometimes one spouse will intentionally configure the other spouse's device with their iCloud account, thereby effectively tapping all of their data. Bottom line . . . don't share your iCloud account credentials. We see this method of data "sniffing" far more often than the installation of spyware or other monitoring software.

Flash Drives

USB flash drives are those small portable devices that attorneys (and others too) use to transfer data between computers. They are also known as thumb drives. They are inexpensive and vary in capacity from several GB up to several hundred GB of storage space. Since they are portable and small, it is very easy to lose them. This is where encryption is your friend. If you intend to store confidential client information on a flash drive, make sure that the device is encrypted. Some encryption software for your computer can also be used to encrypt the flash drive. There are also flash drives that have built-in encryption capabilities. The DataTraveler and IronKey series from Kingston are good choices for encrypted flash drives. If you are a Windows 10 Professional users, don't forget that you can use BitLocker to Go (included free with the operating system) to encrypt any flash drive.

Final Thoughts

The options and requirements for mobile security have certainly changed quickly over the years. Talk to us next year and we're sure the world will have changed again. For now, make sure that you are aware of all the issues related to secure data transfer and that you are not relying on antiquated knowledge. You must assume that there is absolutely no protection of the communication stream between your laptop and whatever you are connecting to. We've seen hotel networks that didn't have a firewall, so all traffic was allowed to flow through. We immediately saw probing attacks on our computers, which were stopped by the firewalls on our laptops. It's the wild, wild West out there, and you're the only marshal in town. Good luck, Wyatt.

CHAPTER TWENTY

Email Providers

Arguably, the most used technology for any attorney is email. The default communication method is sending electronic messages instead of breaking out the typewriter and postage stamp. And most of the profession prefers email to any other kind of electronic communication. That may change, but not yet. Although we are seeing an increase in collaboration communication such as Slack and text messages, email is still king.

What are some of the considerations when choosing an email provider? Is the communication secure? What devices can access the messages? You'll also need to consider if there are any limitations for the email such as attachment size, attachment type, fonts, color, and so on. Sending large attachments could be an issue for some attorneys. If your email system has a low threshold for attachment size, you'll need some sort of file sharing system to collaborate or distribute the information. You may want to consider investigating Citrix ShareFile for securely sharing files instead of sending them as attachments. Another alternative is to implement the Large File Send option in Mimecast, where you can set additional attachment options such as expiration time, printing restrictions, and so on.

Microsoft Exchange

By far, the most popular mechanism to handle email is Microsoft Exchange. Many solo and small firm attorneys host Exchange on their own network while others use a hosted Exchange system with a third party provider. Having your own Exchange server gives you a lot of flexibility. You have total control over the configuration of the Exchange server. As an example, you can increase the attachment size that is allowed, define distribution groups, create rules that automatically take action with messages and control mail flow for alternate services such as automated metadata removal.

By default, Exchange will attempt to send messages using TLS (Transport Layer Security), which is an encrypted communications channel. You have the option of enforcing the TLS connection as well. This means that if you have a sensitive matter, you can configure Exchange to always use TLS when communicating with a particular domain or email address. This would ensure that any message you send to that domain or email address would be encrypted.

Exchange also includes some basic security controls for mobile devices. You should configure the Exchange ActiveSync Mailbox Policies to enforce certain requirements. You can require a password, which is an absolute must. When you require a password, other options become available such as alphanumeric password, require encryption, require encryption on storage card, number of failed attempts allowed, minimum password length, maximum inactivity timer, and password expiration. If you have Exchange Enterprise client access licenses (additional cost and add-on), you can then restrict the usage of certain features. You can allow or prevent the usage of removable storage, camera, Wi-Fi, internet sharing from device, remote desktop from device, and so on. The base level security features (e.g., password policies) are included with Exchange for no additional cost.

Having your own Exchange server does mean hardware and software expense, although it can be very affordable when dealing with virtualized servers. It also comes with the advantage and flexibility of integrating with other applications. As an example, having your own Exchange server tends to make it easier to integrate your email with your practice management software.

Office 365

Each year we continue to see more and more solo and small firm attorneys moving to Office 365. There are a lot of different offerings for Office 365. If you are looking to abandon your local Exchange server, you can purchase a subscription that includes email provided by Exchange. If you only want Exchange and not the Office products, take a look at the Exchange Online Plans. There are other online Exchange products as well such as Online Archiving, Online Protection, and Online Advanced Threat Protection. The bottom line is that Microsoft has a lot of options for the solo and small firm attorney from basic email only to full-function office suites, analytics, advanced e-discovery tools, and much more.

Office 365 seems to be the choice among solo and small firm attorneys, especially when it's time to upgrade their physical Exchange server. After analyzing the cost of new server hardware and license costs for Exchange, the business case usually suggests that moving to Office 365 is the best course of action. Office 365 puts the burden on Microsoft to provide a secure high availability service. That's something most solo and small firm lawyers can't do.

Gmail

We see a lot of solo and small firm lawyers using Gmail as their email address. While it is totally functional, it is not very professional in appearance. We believe that we are now at the time where every lawyer's email address should be associated with a domain name. Forget about an email address from Hotmail (Outlook.com), AOL, Yahoo, and the like. Use of such addresses is a virtual billboard saying that you are not a modern attorney.

Using the free Gmail from Google is not where you want to be even though Google has stopped scanning your email to deliver targeted ads. You should be using G Suite since it provides more reliable, secure communications in addition to productivity tools. With G Suite you can also have an email address associated with your domain name even though Google is providing the service. This means you can have an email address such as yourname@yourlawfirm.com. Now doesn't that look a lot more professional than a Gmail address?

Other Email Providers

There are a lot of providers of email services for the taking. Consider how you would access the email. Is it a POP (Post Office Protocol) account, where you have to download the message to your local computer? POP accounts are a problem if you need to access your mailbox from multiple devices. The sent and received items aren't the same across the various computers and mobile devices. IMAP (Internet Message Access Protocol) is a better type of email account and will maintain synchronized items across all devices.

Even better solutions are some sort of hosted Exchange where you use Outlook to access the mailbox that contains your email, calendar entries, tasks, contacts, and so on. That way all the data stays on the provider's server, which you just access using the mail client from any device. No matter which provider you select, make sure that the provider does not automatically delete suspected spam messages. The system should allow you the opportunity to review any possible spam message (typically in a separate mail area) with the capability to release any false positives.

Additional Email Considerations

When considering an email provider, you should also address spam control, encryption capabilities, potential archiving, threat protection (e.g., viruses, malicious links, malware attachments), and metadata removal. You may be able to address these functions with the email provider or it may steer you toward hosting your own Exchange server in order to control how each item is configured. Third-party vendors can also provide some or all of these services.

If you have your own Exchange server, inbound email is routed through a provider that scans the messages and attachments for any malicious code. The message is then delivered to your server or blocked if it is infected. Outbound messages are sent to the provider for processing as well. They may scan for malicious attachments or provide the ability to encrypt the email.

Some systems have the ability to provide URL protection too. The URL in the message is changed to route through the provider's servers. The provider then inspects the URL to see if it is malicious or has the ability to deposit malware on your machine. Clicking the modified URL sends you to the third-party provider. If the URL is "clean," you will be rerouted to the original destination. If the URL is suspicious or determined to be malicious, a warning panel will be displayed before sending you to the original destination or access will be totally blocked for known malicious sites.

As you can see, there are a lot of things to be considered when choosing an email provider.

CHAPTER TWENTY-ONE

Backup

Backup is an essential operation for every law firm. In fact, adequate backup is implicit in the ABA Model Rules for Professional Conduct and their state counterparts. One of the lawyer's duties is to competently represent clients. How can you do that if your case files and communications are lost? You could have a hardware failure of your server or a disk crash. What if your cloud provider shut its doors, rendering client data inaccessible? Perhaps your laptop is stolen from your vehicle with client data for a pending matter. What if your office internet connection goes down? How will you access your data in the cloud? There are all kinds of situations where you could lose data or not be able to access it. That is where backup comes into play. Should you have a catastrophe, you would restore data from your backup and continue operations.

These days, the threat of ransomware is foremost in many attorneys' minds. If you aren't familiar with ransomware, basically, ransomware is malware that encrypts your data with an encryption key that you do not have. You must pay the ransom in order to get the decryption key and hence access to your data. The sad reality is that even though you pay the ransom, you may not get the decryption key. The latest FBI statistics are that you will get a valid decryption key in less than 50 percent of the cases.

In order to recover from a ransomware attack, backup is your friend. If you are unlucky enough to contract ransomware, just restore your data back from your backups. Of course this implies that you have good backups and have done test restores to make sure you could actually recover from an attack or failure.

External USB Drives

Many solo and small firm attorneys use external USB drives for their backup. That is a perfectly good solution, but disconnect the drive once the backup is completed. Also, you should have at least two backup drives in case one of them is connected at the same time your computer experiences a ransomware infection. At least two drives is also a requirement as you may have a hardware failure of one of the drives. Using a cloud-based backup solution will also allow you to restore data following a ransomware attack. Just like the external USB drives, make sure you have at least two backup sets in the cloud.

Hopefully your computer is equipped with a USB 3.0 port, which will allow for faster backups due to the faster transfer speeds versus a USB 2.0 connection. That means you should be only looking at purchasing an external USB 3.0 hard drive. You may want to consider getting a USB drive with built-in hardware encryption. Hardware encryption will ensure that the data is protected when the device is disconnected and powered off.

Many external USB drives also come with backup software. NovaBackup and Acronis True Image are good backup software products that can be used to back up your computer to any external USB drive.

An even better external drive solution is a small NAS (Network Attached Storage) device such as the Buffalo LinkStation 220. The LinkStation 220 holds two hard drives, which can be configured as RAID 1. RAID 1 mirrors the drives, thereby providing redundancy if one hard disk fails. The combined cost of the LinkStation will be slightly higher than two separate USB drives, but you get the added advantage of having redundancy is a single case. The downside is that you need to purchase two units so that you can have one stored off-site in case something happens to your physical office.

Whether you use external USB drives or a NAS, supplementing with cloud storage gives you lots of flexibility in how you engineer your backup solution.

Backup Appliance

Another solution is to use an onsite backup appliance that is agent-based. This means that you install a software agent on the computer to be backed up and data is transferred over the network to the appliance by using the agent. Typically, the backup appliance solution is used to backup local servers. The software is configured to periodically take snapshots of the server and stores the backup data on the appliance. In addition, consider sending an encrypted version of the backup data to the cloud. Some appliances have the ability to virtualize the server should the actual physical server suffer a hardware or software failure. As an example, the backup appliances that we implement can take snapshots every 15 minutes and virtualize a server within a few hours.

Cloud Backup

There are many good backup solutions using the cloud. If possible, you should look to a cloud provider that allows you to control the encryption key used to encrypt the data. User defined encryption keys mean that the cloud provider cannot decrypt the data even though they can access it. Carbonite is a good backup cloud provider that has that capability. A best practice would be to have multiple versions of the backup data in the cloud. That way, if one gets corrupted or suffers a ransomware infection, you'll have alternate backup sets to restore from. Other highly reviewed backup providers are CloudBerry and Backblaze.

Target Data

Selecting the appropriate technology is just one piece of the backup puzzle. The first thing you need to do is determine what you will back up. If you are looking for a disaster recovery option (total loss of equipment or service), you'll need a method that will allow you to recover quickly and preserve not just the data, but possibly applications as well. You'll probably end up with some sort of backup appliance if disaster recovery is your goal.

Risk Assessment

Once you have determined what needs to be protected, the next analysis is to determine the likelihood of data loss or inaccessibility. How likely is there to be a hardware failure? Perhaps your risk is fairly low if you have new hardware. However, failures can occur beyond hardware issues. Data could become corrupted. Someone could inadvertently delete a file. You could overwrite a file with the wrong version thereby destroying the original contents and of course, ransomware could render data inaccessible.

No matter what the scenario, you should perform a risk assessment and determine action steps to mitigate that risk.

Data Location

Another consideration is data location. Where is your important data being held? Many lawyers still have on premise equipment and keep their data on local storage devices. They just don't trust losing control of the data by putting it in the hands of a third party. Others are using cloud services and confidential client data is out of the lawyer's direct control. Different methods are needed if you have direct access to the data or it resides on some external service.

No matter where the data resides, the challenge is to find it all. You would be surprised at all the places law firm data ends up. Employees take data home. It exists on flash drives. It may be sent as attachments to a personal web-based email account. Spend a little time to inventory all or the data sources. You can't back it up if you don't know you have it. "Dark data"—data a law firm doesn't know it has—has grown by leaps and bounds in recent years. It presents all kinds of risks—you can't protect that data, you can't back it up and if you don't know you have it, you may fail to disclose it when required to do so by laws and regulations or in litigation.

What about personal devices such as smartphones? You'll have to decide if the information on a personal device is at risk of being lost and should be backed up. This may be a good time to rethink your BYOD (Bring Your Own Device) policy and what devices can access firm data. If you do decide that smartphone information needs to be backed up, there are software solutions to accomplish this. Should you leave the process up to each individual or should you invest in a MDM (Mobile Device Management) system?

How Much?

Finally, how much data do you need to back up? That can radically impact your backup strategy. Hard drive space is fairly cheap these days, but you can't defy the laws of physics. Transfer times are only so fast. You can't make the electrons move any faster. Network speeds will limit the amount of data transfer as well. Perhaps now is a good time to upgrade your network cabling and hardware. If you are only backing up to the cloud, hard drive space is not an issue. However, you will need to know the data volume in order to determine how much the off-site storage is going to cost.

Final Thoughts

We worry about backup for lots of reasons. The natural disasters of 2017 and 2018 were a great reminder of the need for having backups, as many lawyers painfully discovered.

Beyond that, ransomware has been on a wild roller-coaster ride, causing havoc everywhere, including in law firms. Ransomware really is a global epidemic today. The "bad guys" are constantly updating code and discovering new vulnerabilities to exploit. We hope you never have to experience a ransomware event. But if you do, make sure you have properly engineered your backup so you can get back in business with minimal effort and pain. Engineering a good backup system is one of the smartest things any law firm can do to protect its confidential data.

CHAPTER TWENTY-TWO

Tomorrow in Legal Tech

"You can kill stupid rules. You can kill stupid meetings. You CANNOT kill stupid people."

—Mary Abraham

Introduction

We love that quote. We think the reality of Mary's words, taken from a review of the keynote at ILTACON 2018, has finally hit home with the C-Suite. No amount of technology can protect you from your employees, who are simultaneously your greatest asset and your greatest threat. So let's start with some of the developments in the legal sector which revolve around cybersecurity.

Cybersecurity

Employee Security Awareness Training

In 2017, we did a fair number of employee security awareness trainings. In 2018, those trainings constituted about half of our presentations. We expect the sheer number of such presentations to rise again next year. So yes, the C-Suite has heard and realized that Mary is right. Roughly 4 percent of law firm employees are invariably the repeat offenders who click on an attachment or a link within a phishing email. Since you can't kill them, you must educate them—and on a regular basis because threats and tactics evolve quickly.

A report from cybersecurity leader FireEye, in which over half a billion emails sent between January and June 2018 were analyzed, found that one in every

101 emails is malicious and intended to compromise a user or network. If you take away the spam, only one-third of emails are regarded as "clean."

In 2018, Barracuda published a study of 3000 business email compromise (BEC) attacks. These attacks are often called CEO fraud because the CEO's identity is most often impersonated. The attacks succeed due to the simplicity and urgency of the attacks according to the study which also noted that 60 percent of the email attacks did not contain a phishing link. Most simply began a conversation which convinced the employee that the sender was real—and then requested the transfer of monies or W2 information which was then used to fraudulently file tax returns and collect refunds.

So in your training, make sure you include the FBI's recommendation on defending against BEC attacks: "The best way to avoid being exploited is to verify the authenticity of requests to send money by walking into the CEO's office or speaking to him or her directly on the phone. Don't rely on email alone." More helpful advice can be found at https://www.fbi.gov/news/stories/business-e-mail-compromise-on-the-rise.

A Hot for Security post from Bitdefender reported on a survey of 2000 users by the password management experts at LogMeIn. Ninety-one percent of people know that password recycling poses huge security risks, yet 59 percent still use the same password everywhere. They know better but they still do it. The number one reason for password reuse is fear of forgetfulness. Number two was wanting to know and be in control of all their passwords, which is certainly made simpler by only having one. Good heavens.

And in bad news for businesses, 47 percent say there is no difference in passwords created for personal and work accounts. Only 19 percent are more careful with their work login details, and 38 percent never use the same password for work and personal accounts. Unfortunately, the other 62 percent do.

Seventy-two percent feel well informed on password best practices (though the survey results don't bear that out), but 64 percent of those also prefer a password that's easy to remember, and they admitted they always choose convenience over security. That part is certainly not news.

What is it that Forrest Gump said? Stupid is as stupid does.

NIST (The National Institute of Standards and Technology) released in July of 2018 a draft guidebook called *Cybersecurity is Everyone's Job*. It is certainly hard to argue with the title! The guidebook was created for business owners and leaders, but it's also helpful for those serving functional roles in human resources (HR), IT, legal—and even sales and marketing. The final guidebook may well be published by the time you read this, so be sure to search for the final version.

Undeniably, employees represent the "largest attack surface" of most organizations. Common business activities—such as product and service delivery, payroll, accounts payable, communicating with customers and suppliers and resource management—frequently expose organizations to cyber risk, which is why a cybersecurity culture is so critical.

Mindset is also a key driver of human behavior—so proper attention must be paid to evaluating and addressing employees' mindsets (they must be persuaded that they can't sacrifice security for convenience) as part of a broader security-awareness campaign. Also, due to the rise in attacks leveraging social engineering, organizations should seek to educate their employees about such attacks and thereby "harden" their security. Hardening the technology is (sigh) a lot easier.

The guidebook's recommendations for action include:

- Understanding cybersecurity well enough to enable sound decision making;
- Including cyber risks in the enterprise risk management (ERM) process;
- Developing and maintaining organizational information security policies and standards;
- Promoting the development of effective cross-functional teams to accomplish cybersecurity goals for the organization; and
- Protecting sensitive strategic, financial, legal and risk information.

It's only 26 pages, which is not terribly intimidating—and it may be very helpful to those who do not yet have a cohesive plan for addressing cybersecurity.

Account Takeover Attacks on the Rise

More than three-quarters of Account Takeover Attacks (ATOs) resulted in a phishing email, a 2018 report from Barracuda showed.

Why spoof an email address for phishing messages when you can hijack an account and send them from the real one? Barracuda checked with 50 randomly selected organizations—nearly 40 percent of respondents reported at least one ATO attack in the second quarter of 2018. "On average, when a company got compromised, the compromise resulted in at least three separate account takeover incidents," according to the report. Of the incidents, 78 percent resulted in phishing emails being sent.

The percentage is probably higher since the survey was based on incidents reported by companies. Many companies don't know they've been attacked—and others may not want to 'fess up to being victims. ATOs really do appear to come from (say) the CEO and so, if well crafted, they really can get an employee to click on an attachment or link—or give up company secrets. Cautioning employees about these attacks has become a critical component in employee security training.

Office 365 May Not Be as Secure as You Think

How secure is your implementation of Office 365?

Lawyers look at us blankly when we ask that question. But it is a question posed by Microsoft itself, which says on its website, "Ever wonder how secure your Office 365 organization really is? Time to stop wondering—the Office 365 Secure Score is here to help. Secure Score analyzes your Office 365 organization's security based on your regular activities and security settings and assigns a score. Think of it as a credit score for security." https://support.office.com/en-gb/article/introducing-the-office-365-secure-score-c9e7160f-2c34-4bd0-a548-5ddcc862eaef

Office 365 isn't magically secure out of the gate. It needs some help from your end. Secure Score looks at the Office 365 services you use and then looks at your settings and activities before assigning you a score that represents the quality of your security practices.

When we get a new client that is using Office 365, it is standard practice now to run "Secure Score." And the results are usually dreadful. You don't have to reach the pinnacle here—as we always say, the object is to "get to good."

Similar scoring is available for Windows 10. As we go to print, Microsoft is continuously evolving Secure Score—including its exact name, but searching for the product and the words "Secure Score" should produce the most current results. 2019 is likely to see further rapidly changing developments of Secure Score—so keep an eye out.

Developments from NIST and CIS

The National Institute of Standards and Technology (NIST) announced in April of 2018 that it had released version 1.1 of its popular Framework for Improving Critical Infrastructure Cybersecurity, more widely known as the Cybersecurity Framework. You can—and should—read and implement its recommendations in 2019: https://nvlpubs.nist.gov/nistpubs/CSWP/NIST.CSWP.04162018.pdf

The Center for Internet Security released a new version of its Top 20 Controls in 2018. We think of NIST as the "what" and CIS as the "how." The controls can be found at https://www.cisecurity.org/controls/.

NIST also released its Small Business Cybersecurity Guide which can be found at https://nvlpubs.nist.gov/nistpubs/ir/2016/NIST.IR.7621r1.pdf.

Taken together, these three documents, which are relatively short and easily comprehended, will go a very long way toward helping solo and small law firms become secure.

IBM Security: Cybersecurity Still a Critical Challenge for Businesses

In March of 2018, IBM Security published the results of a new global study on organizational cybersecurity readiness and resiliency entitled "The 2018 Cyber Resilient Organization." The survey was conducted by the Ponemon Institute and can be found at https://info.resilientsystems.com/hubfs/IBM_Resilient_Branded_Content/White_Papers/2018_Cyber_Resilient_Organization_Study.pdf. It includes insights from more than 2,800 security and IT professionals, and establishes that cybersecurity readiness remains a critical challenge for businesses worldwide. Some of the major findings:

- 77 percent of respondents admit they do not have a formal cybersecurity incident response plan applied consistently across their organization;
- 77 percent of respondents report having difficulty retaining and hiring quality IT security professionals;
- 50 percent of respondents believe their incident response plan is either informal, ad hoc, or non-existent;
- 60 percent of respondents consider lack of investment in artificial intelligence and machine learning as the biggest barrier to achieving cyber resilience;
- 31 percent of respondents believe they have an adequate cybersecurity budget in place;
- 29 percent of respondents report having ideal staffing to achieve cyber resilience; and
- 23 percent of respondents say they do not currently have a CISO or security leader.

These results pretty much track the results of PricewaterhouseCoopers' Global State of Information Security Survey (GSISS) 2018, which found that of the more than 9,500 senior executives surveyed in 122 countries:

- 67 percent have an internet of things (IoT) security strategy in place or are currently implementing one;
- 36 percent have uniform cybersecurity standards and policies for IoT devices and systems;
- 34 percent have new data collection, retention and destruction policies; and
- 34 percent assess device and system interconnectivity and vulnerability across the business ecosystem.

As you read the findings, consider where you need to place the emphasis in your law firm. Every year, you need to be improving your security posture.

2018 Corporate Counsel Breach Statistics—Prepare to Groan

Here's the news in a nutshell: Data breaches of in-house legal departments have doubled in the last year. Assuming that elicited a groan, the source is the 2018 survey by the Association for Corporate Counsel, which reported one-third of in-house counsel offices experienced a data breach in 2017, up from 15 percent in 2016. That's a significant rise.

An *ABA Journal* article quoted Sterling Miller, general counsel of Marketo Inc., an online marketing technology company: "The possibility that your outside law firm could be breached and your sensitive data stolen is a huge nightmare for in-house lawyers. Outside counsel need to start taking this very seriously. If a breach happens, that law firm is probably no longer working for you and the malpractice claim could be very large."

It doesn't really matter whether you are in-house or outside counsel—the odds are, as stated above, that you need to up your security game.

That ABA article analyzed the ABA TechReport 2017 and found that "only 26 percent of responding firms had an incident response plan in place to address a security breach, and only two-thirds with 500 lawyers or more had such a plan in place. These plans were not a priority with smaller firms, as 31 percent of firms with 10 to 49 lawyers, 14 percent of firms with two to nine lawyers, and 10 percent of solo practices had such plans."

The high profile cybersecurity firm Mandiant, a division of FireEye, estimates that 80 of the top 100 law firms (by revenue) have been hacked since 2011. Our private conversations with large firm lawyers seem to bear out that estimation.

It appears that lawyers everywhere have some serious cybersecurity shoring up to do. There were a lot of cybersecurity projections this year—but then cybersecurity is white hot as security incidents—and breaches—proliferate at an alarming rate. 2019 is not going to be any better!

The Decline of Ransomware and the Rise of Cryptocurrency Mining

In 2017, ransomware was in all the headlines. But ransomware, while still around, is actually declining according to a 2018 Kaspersky Security Network report documenting a 30 percent decline in ransomware attacks between April 2017 and March 2018 compared with the same period the previous year. A 2018 threat report by McAfee Labs also suggests a drop in the detection of ransomware attacks—putting the decline at 32 percent.

A key factor behind the decline is the rise of cryptocurrency mining malware and low-level cyber criminals shifting their attention to 'cryptojacking' as a simpler, less risky way of making money. And the criminals come after law firms, just as they do everyone else.

These cryptojacking attacks involve attackers infecting a PC with malware which secretly uses the PC's processing power to mine for cryptocurrency—usually the relatively simple-to-mine Monero—a small portion of which is deposited into their own wallet. Another method of cryptojacking is infecting a website and inserting JavaScript code to do the mining. Visitors to the website silently execute the JavaScript code to generate the cryptocurrency. No client software installation required. Unlike ransomware, it's stealthy and as long as the infection isn't discovered, it will continue to deliver the attacker a steady stream of income. The subtle nature of the attack has boosted the popularity of cryptojacking throughout 2018—and there is no reason to think it won't continue to grow in 2019. So long as the cybercriminals are smart and don't use up too many of your computing resources, you'll never know a thing. If you want to know how to prevent cryptojacking, there is a lot of useful information at https://www.csoonline.com/article/3253572/internet/what-is-cryptojacking-how-to-prevent-detect-and-recover-from-it.html

The European Union's General Data Protection Regulation

The EU General Data Protection Regulation (GDPR) took the legal world by storm when it became effective in May 25, 2018. Many law firms will still be scrambling in 2019 to become compliant with the GDPR.

IT Governance had a helpful post with free (your favorite price) resources to help you comply with the European Union's General Data Protection Regulation (GDPR) which requires all organizations that handle, store, and process the data of EU residents' data to abide by its strict terms. You can find the list of resources at https://www.itgovernanceusa.com/blog/list-of-free-gdpr-resources/.

The fines for non-compliance can be onerous, so this is not a task you should defer. Smaller law firms may have less exposure, but it is amazing how many small law firms do indeed hold, store or process the data of EU residents. By the way, it appears that you can only protect yourself against the fines (typically via insurance) in two EU countries—the others nations prohibit doing so.

Say Hello to Norman, the World's First 'Psychopathic' AI

We continue to follow the growth of AI in the legal sector—it made some nice progress in 2018 and we expect more in 2019. But when we read about Norman, the world's first psychopathic AI, we concluded that a whole lot of worrying was justified. It seemed likely to us that Norman was named for Norman Bates in the movie *Psycho*.

Researchers at the Massachusetts Institute of Technology (MIT) developed Norman. Their experiment was based on the 1921 Rorschach test, which identifies traits in humans deemed to be psychopathic based on their perception of inkblots, along with what is known as thought disorders.

Norman is an AI experiment who was given "extended exposure to the darkest corners of Reddit," according to MIT, in order to explore how datasets and bias can influence the behavior and decisionmaking capabilities of artificial intelligence.

"When people talk about AI algorithms being biased and unfair, the culprit is often not the algorithm itself, but the biased data that was fed to it," the researchers say. "The same method can see very different things in an image, even sick things, if trained on the wrong (or, the right!) data set." We couldn't agree more.

Norman is an AI system trained to perform image captioning, in which deep learning algorithms are used to generate a text description of an image. As you might imagine, since Norman was exposed to the depths of Reddit and a select subreddit dedicated to graphic content full of images of death and destruction, his datasets are a world away from what a standard AI is normally trained on.

In a stunning example of artificial intelligence gone wrong, MIT performed the Rorschach inkblot tests on Norman, with a standard image captioning neural network used as a control subject for comparison.

Prepared to be disturbed.

In one inkblot test, a standard AI saw "a black and white photo of a red and white umbrella," while Norman saw "man gets electrocuted while attempting to cross busy street."

In another, the control AI described the inkblot as "a black and white photo of a small bird," whereas Norman described the image as "man gets pulled into dough machine."

Norman's perceptions were downright alarming.

Trying to be as ethical as possible, MIT only introduced bias in relation to image captions from the subreddit which are later matched with randomly generated inkblots. To put it another way, the researchers did not use true images of people dying during the experiment. Scant comfort there, given how Norman saw the inkblots. We can only imagine what he would have reported the images to be if he had seen true images of death.

In one way, we shouldn't be surprised—our AI systems have already proven to be fraught with human biases. But this experiment highlights the need for an ethical approach to AI. With poor datasets, you cannot rely on the decisions an AI system makes—and you can alter its perception of the world.

Will someone (including nation states) deliberately make an evil AI? Of course they will. It's what humans do. Someone, as Elon Musk might say, will summon the devil. We darn well better get a firm handle on the ethics of AI before that happens. And we have already proven that bias is inherent in AI "black boxes" (where no one knows how the proprietary system works) that advise judges on sentencing guidelines. If you want to read about that, here's an excellent article from *The New York Times*: https://www.nytimes.com/2017/10/26/opinion/algorithm-compas-sentencing-bias.html.

We will continue to watch the intersection between AI and the law in 2019 with fascination and trepidation.

The Cloudy Forecast for Cloud Computing

Cloud computing still causes unease for some lawyers, but the anxiety is lessening, especially as lawyers are moving in droves to Office 365. At this point, they just can't get to the cloud fast enough. Still, there are issues. In April of 2018, thousands of users couldn't log into Office 365—we can only imagine what would have happened if this happened to lawyers (unless they had the data stored locally).

The problem was largely abroad, but what if it had happened here? Many users were out of business. The cause was an authentication issue which Microsoft resolved pretty quickly. But for those who didn't have a backup solution for email and other functions, they were out of luck until the fix came.

Everywhere we lecture, we continue to get cloud questions. Yes, you should be backing up to the cloud—multiple instances of backup are required. Yes, the cloud is ethical to use, so long as you do your due diligence in selecting a cloud vendor.

Along those lines, *The National Law Review* made recommendations in an article for selecting a cloudbased vendor in April of 2018. Below are some of their recommendations along with our own.

One of the best ways to vet a vendor is to ask for references of businesses similar to yours (e.g. other law firms) who use their platform. If the vendor doesn't have any, that's a warning flag.

Outline best practices and protocols that every vendor must meet. Some of the larger clouds don't negotiate, but many smaller cloud providers will. If you can, bring in a security consultant to help write requirements documentation. You can also gather data from similar businesses through references and networking to ensure that you have a comprehensive understanding of what legal security requirements are.

Be wary of possible snake oil in the vendor's sales pitch.

Here are some questions that the article suggests you ask:

- Where is the data stored?
- What level of vetting do the company's employees go through?
- Is data encrypted every step of the way?
- Are all systems being kept up to date with security patches? How frequently?

- Does the vendor sub-contract any work?
- How is the company structured? Who is legally liable for security breaches?
- How does the vendor's software integrate with your current suite of tools?
- Does the vendor's software allow you to customize the security roles for your firm without having to choose from predetermined options?

Engaging a cloud provider is a major event—it might be wise to bring in an expert to offer guidance if your budget permits it. And read those terms of service as well as any contract you sign—that's where all the devilish details are!!!

Avvo News

It was a big year for Avvo news. And since Avvo is used by many lawyers, it is worth covering that news. Early in 2018, Avvo was acquired by Internet Brands, which also owns Martindale-Hubbell and other legal vertical entities. Internet Brands apparently is risk-adverse and did not want to take on the controversies between state bars and Avvo regarding Avvo legal services and (in particular) fee sharing, which some states believed to be unethical. In June, Internet Brands announced that Avvo Legal Services would be terminated at the end of July, with the remainder of Avvo's functionality remaining intact.

This was an issue we spent a lot of time on in Virginia, concluding that that there could be attorney client matching services which would survive ethical scrutiny—but not the Avvo model. Then, as we were going to print, there was more news.

Many lawyers have railed against Avvo's attorney rating system, which could be artificially pumped up by anyone who could Google "How to Improve Your Avvo Rating." The ratings were seen by many, including the authors, as inherently deceptive and prone to manipulation, some of it actively encouraged by Avvo itself.

So we were delighted when Reuters reported that New York Attorney General Barbara Underwood said that Avvo had agreed, following a probe by her office, to reform its rating system and improve disclosures after the probe revealed shortcomings in how it presented information to consumers seeking to hire lawyers. Specifically, it will no longer call its ratings "unbiased."

She also said Avvo was now "clearly and conspicuously" telling users that its ratings, on a one to ten scale, rely on information that lawyers provide, meaning that lawyers who share their resumes or work experiences tend to rate higher than those who do not.

The attorney general said Avvo also agreed to remove ratings for lawyers who do not actively participate in its directory, and will ensure that forms it posts for consumers are first reviewed by qualified, licensed lawyers in New York.

Avvo will also pay $50,000 to cover costs. In a statement, Avvo said it was committed to providing "timely, accurate information" to help people find lawyers, and the changes reflected its "commitment to pro-consumer practices and improving the accessibility of the legal community."

The news from New York was good news. But as much as we have been disturbed by some of Avvo's practices in the past, we are genuinely pleased that Avvo moved many bars forward in their thinking, because attorney client matching services, ethically constructed, could certainly assist in providing better access to justice.

ABA Issues New Ethics Opinion on the Duties of Lawyers Following a Disaster

Yes, this does have a legal tech component, and especially as we write this with Hurricane Michael having just hit Florida causing all kinds of devastation. The ABA released ABA Formal Ethics Opinion 482 on September 19, 2018. The opinion may be found at https://www.americanbar.org/content/dam/aba/administrative/professional_responsibility/aba_formal_opinion_482.authcheckdam.pdf.

In the opinion, the Standing Committee on Ethics and Professional Responsibility clarifies the ethical obligations attorneys face when disaster strikes.

Lawyers must follow the duty of communication required by Rule 1.4 of the ABA Model Rules of Professional Conduct, which requires lawyers to communicate regularly with clients and to keep clients reasonably apprised of their cases. Following a disaster, a lawyer must evaluate available methods to maintain communication with clients. The opinion instructs that lawyers should keep electronic lists of current clients in a manner that is "easily accessible."

Lawyers should pay attention to the duty of competency, Rule 1.1, which includes a technology clause that requires lawyers to consider the benefits and risks of relevant technology. Because a disaster can destroy lawyers' paper files, lawyers "must evaluate in advance storing files electronically" so that they can access those files after a disaster. Storing client files through cloud technology requires lawyers to consider confidentially obligations.

With a little due diligence, this should not present much of a problem. We constantly encourage lawyers to keep backups in the cloud. It is prudent to have a local backup, but the cloud provides additional security. As we learned from Katrina, having a backup at the office and one at home a mile away is not sufficiently protecting confidential data.

If a disaster causes the loss of client files, lawyers must also consider their ethical obligations under Rule 1.15, which requires lawyers to safeguard client property. For current clients, lawyers can attempt first to reconstruct files by obtaining documents from other sources. If they cannot, lawyers must notify the clients of the loss of files or property. To prevent such losses, "lawyers should maintain an electronic copy of important documents in an off-site location that is updated regularly." Yup, we're back to the cloud again.

A disaster could impact financial institutions and, therefore, client funds. Thus, lawyers "must take reasonable steps in the event of a disaster to ensure access to funds the lawyer is holding in trust." It struck us that this could be highly problematic in some circumstances, but of course it is wise to do whatever one can.

A disaster may cause an attorney to have to withdraw from a client's case under Rule 1.16. "In determining whether withdrawal is required, lawyers must assess whether the client needs immediate legal services that the lawyer will be unable to timely provide," the opinion notes. We certainly saw a lot of withdrawals after Katrina. Entire law practices closed their doors, some forever.

The opinion also warns lawyers that they should not take advantage of disaster victims for personal gain: "Of particular concern is the possibility of improper solicitation in the wake of a disaster." Ambulance chasers, hurricane and flooding chasers—all distasteful, but they've been with us for a long time.

On balance, the opinion provides some good guidance and may help lawyers to form an incident response plan that complies with the guidance of this opinion. It's worth taking a look at your incident response plan to see if modifications are warranted. And if you don't have a formal incident response plan, this is a good time to formulate one! At a recent CLE with some 40 attendees, only a single attendee had a written incident response plan. We need to do better than that—put that high on your agenda for 2019.

ABA Issues New Ethics Opinion on Ethical Duties Following a Data Breach or Cyberattack

On October 17, 2018, the ABA issued Formal Opinion 484, Lawyers' Obligations After an Electronic Data Breach or Cyberattack which may be found at https://www.americanbar.org/content/dam/aba/administrative/professional_responsibility/aba_formal_op_483.pdf.

This opinion builds on the standing committee's Formal Opinion 477R released in May 2017, which set forth a lawyer's ethical obligation to secure protected client information when communicating digitally.

The new opinion states: "When a breach of protected client information is either suspected or detected, Rule 1.1 requires that the lawyer act reasonably and promptly to stop the breach and mitigate damage resulting from the breach."

The ethics opinion implicates Model Rule 1.1 (competence), Model Rule 1.4 (communications), Model Rule 1.6 (confidentiality of information), Model Rule 1.15 (safekeeping property), Model Rule 5.1 (responsibilities of a partner or supervisory lawyer) and Model Rule 5.3 (responsibilities regarding nonlawyer assistance).

There is a "rule of reason" overtone to the opinion, which states, "As a matter of preparation and best practices, however, lawyers should consider proactively developing an incident response plan with specific plans and procedures for responding to a data breach," states the opinion. "The decision whether to adopt a plan, the content of any plan and actions taken to train and prepare for implementation of the plan should be made before a lawyer is swept up in an actual breach."

This is of course what cybersecurity experts have said for a very long time—and, in our experience, all large firms tend to have an incident response plan. The smaller firms? Not so much.

The opinion also recommends, in a footnote, that firms should have data retention policies that limit their possession of personally identifiable information. We certainly agree with that. Lots of firms have "zombie" data—data they don't know they have until there is a data breach.

Since data breaches cannot entirely be avoided, the opinion says, "When they do (have a breach), they have a duty to notify clients of the data breach under Model Rule 1.4 in sufficient detail to keep clients 'reasonably informed' and with an explanation 'to the extent necessary to permit the client to make informed decisions regarding the representation.'"

Staying Current on Legal Tech

It isn't easy staying current on legal technology. And lawyers have billable hours (and many required non-billable hours) to contend with. One of our favorite resources is *Attorney at Work*, a website which gives you a tip each day. https://www.attorneyatwork.com/. Not all the tips are about technology, but many are—and the other tips can be incredibly helpful with management, financial and marketing issues. This is a free publication. Just subscribe via email. If the tip of the day doesn't interest you, just hit delete—the subject line alone will tell you.

Legal Talk Network has a wealth of podcasts to listen to—again, not all are related to technology, but many are. https://legaltalknetwork.com/. We are particularly fond of the *Kennedy-Mighell Report* and (of course), *The Digital Edge*, which author Nelson co-hosts with Jim Calloway.

Don't overlook the value of attending legal tech CLEs—just make sure they have good speakers, knowledgeable on legal tech, and able to entertain as well as inform you. Ask colleagues for referrals—and while live CLE is always the best, there are plenty of good webinars, many available on demand. Your state bar probably has them and certainly the ABA has a wealth of legal tech webinars on demand at Shop ABA. https://www.americanbar.org/products/.

Finally, there was a major development this year as Bob Ambrogi signed off on his Lawyer2Lawyer podcast and launched his new podcast, *LawNext*. https://lawnext.com/. We have faithfully followed Bob for years—he is always a reliable source of very current legal tech info. His LawSites blog is our go-to legal tech resource. https://www.lawsitesblog.com/. Again, if you subscribe, the subject line of your daily email will tell you at once whether this is a post you want to read. We wish Bob well in his new podcast and offer gratitude for all of the invaluable information he has provided to the legal profession over many years—we look forward to 2019 and seeing how he continues to amaze us by having his finger on the pulse of legal tech.

Many Lawyers Need a Digital Detox

There are very few lawyers who seem to have control over their digital devices. To the contrary, the devices themselves seem to be in control, demanding the nearly non-stop attention of lawyers. It might seem odd to hear three geeks talk about digital detoxing, but we recognized the need for it years ago. Perhaps, as geeks, we were on the bleeding edge of this phenomenon.

It's not as though we need a scientist to explain the fundamentals to us. Lawyers tell us all the time that they feel their blood pressure rising as they look at all the unread emails in their Inboxes. They feel phantom phone vibrations in their pockets. They can't go more than a few minutes without checking their phones. They text, email and talk while driving or at stop lights. How many times have you had to honk at someone who doesn't move when the red light goes green? We are amazed at how often this happens in one week's commuting time.

People check their phones an astonishing 47 times each day, on average. According to consulting firm Deloitte, almost half of people check their phones at least once during the night. Nearly two-thirds of us check our phones within 15 minutes of arising in the morning.

Our technology has become an addiction as disturbing as reliance on drugs or alcohol. Many experts say that technology is rewiring our brains and we tend to agree.

In June of 2017, McAfee released a document called "Report: Digital Detox—Unwind, Relax and Unplug"—it is chockablock full of statistics about the extent of our addiction. You can find the report at https://www.mcafee.com/resources/misc/pr-unplugging-study-digital-detox.pdf. As depressing as it may be, it offers support for our conviction that everyone, lawyers included, need to take a long hard look at how their digital devices have changed their lives.

When do lawyers make mistakes? When you move too fast. The news is full of stories of lawyers who sent confidential data to reporters because they were using the "auto-complete" function of Outlook and didn't check the email addresses in "To" field.

The same is true of allowing our devices to constantly distract us. When we cannot concentrate, and allow ourselves to be distracted endlessly by emails or texts, we can hardly expect to be doing our best work.

Likewise, the immediacy of email doesn't give us a chance to cool off. We get an ugly, profanity-laced email and the tendency is to respond in kind rather than taking a walk and cooling off.

A lot of lawyers answer their email at night—and many do so after having several libations. This is never a good idea. All sorts of unintentional mischief may be created. Your judgment may be impacted—and you may not be aware that your judgment has been impacted! And if you are one of those who wakes up in the middle of the night and groggily checks your phone, your odds of operating competently as a lawyer diminish considerably. Being tired or under the influence can lead to ethical infractions you would never ordinarily make.

You don't have to go all the way with digital detoxing. You can take baby steps. If you set aside mealtimes or after dinner as "device-free," you are very likely to find that your stress level (and blood pressure) go down. Most lawyers we know say they regularly feel stressed. Many are on anti-anxiety or anti-depression medications. Disconnecting from the digital world on a regular basis may actually decrease the need for medications. At the very least, the sense of being stressed and overwhelmed goes down.

With all the focus we now see on lawyer "wellness," it is amazing how often digital detoxing comes up—and you can be sure you'll hear much more about it in 2019. So go ahead and make some resolutions about "getting off the grid." You won't regret it.

Index

C

L

M

N

U

V

W